Daylight

Beach Lovers

Erica Reade

Cofounders: Taj Forer and Michael Itkoff
Creative Director: Ursula Damm
Copy Editor: Gabrielle Fastman

© 2022 Daylight Community Arts Foundation

Photographs © 2021 by Erica Reade
www.ericareadeimages.com

Afterword © 2021 by Erica Reade

"Swept Away: The Epic Romance of Beach Life" © 2021 by Gulnara Samoilova

ISBN: 978-1-954119-13-0

Printed by Ofset Yapimevi, Turkey

Daylight Books
E-mail: info@daylightbooks.org
Web: www.daylightbooks.org

O madly the sea pushes upon the land
with love, with love.

—Walt Whitman

Swept Away:
The Epic Romance of Beach Life

In 1992, I left my home in Ufa, the capital of Bashkortostan, and arrived in New York City with a single suitcase and one hundred dollars to my name. Although I knew I would never return to the former Soviet Union, I packed light: a pair of high heels and my negatives. I was ready to start my new life.

A week later, my boyfriend took me on our first American date—to Brighton Beach. I think he was trying to make me feel more at home, but I am Tatar, not Russian, so it was a little strange to suddenly feel like I was back in the USSR. I remember walking along the boardwalk taking in the sights, and then strolling down to the beach. I felt a profound sense of awe and wonder standing on the edge of the earth and seeing the ocean for the very first time in my life.

Watching the waves of the Atlantic crest, their frothy white peaks rise only to crash into the surf, filled me with something I had never felt before. The ocean is always moving, always pushing and pulling at the earth, guided by an internal metronome that always takes the edge off. Whenever I feel bad, I go to Coney Island, sit in front of the ocean, and meditate. The ocean is my escape, a place to connect with nature and realize how small I am in the scope of the universe. Perhaps the beach has this same effect for other New Yorkers too.

I am particularly drawn to beach photography as it reveals the intimate side of people in public space. Here, amid the vast expanses of sand and surf, people can leave their cares—and clothes—behind, and freely frolic, play, and enjoy the simple pleasures of life. New York City beaches have a certain charm you won't find anywhere else, a distinctive mix of high energy, wild style, and joyful outrageousness.

At its best, street photography captures the poetic, lyrical, mysterious, and ambiguous aspects of life, the strange and wonderful things that happen in the blink of an eye. So often we are in public going about our day, then we see something so unlikely or strangely moving that it snaps us out of the monotony of the mundane. It doesn't need to be a "big" moment as a photojournalist would pursue; it's more about discovering the remarkable beauty that surrounds us, should we choose to look.

Erica Reade's photographs do just this, providing us with a lyrical portrait of the simple pleasures of life. Liberated from the strictures of work, responsibilities, and even clothes, on the beach we are free to frolic and play as the children we once were. Reveling in the raptures of the sun and shore, we are whisked away to a better world. Camera in hand, Erica captures it all.

Beach Lovers is about New York at its very best: a place where we are free to live our best lives. The series captured my imagination with its beauty, elegance, and timeless glamour. You can get lost in the moment, swept away, and drawn into another world that makes you feel as if you are starring in a Hollywood film. But this is real. And that is what street photography does best, subtly layering multiple stories in a single frame. In her tender scenes of love on the beach, Erica captures the private pleasures of romance, beauty, and joy lived open and free.

—Gulnara Samoilova
Founder, Women Street Photographers

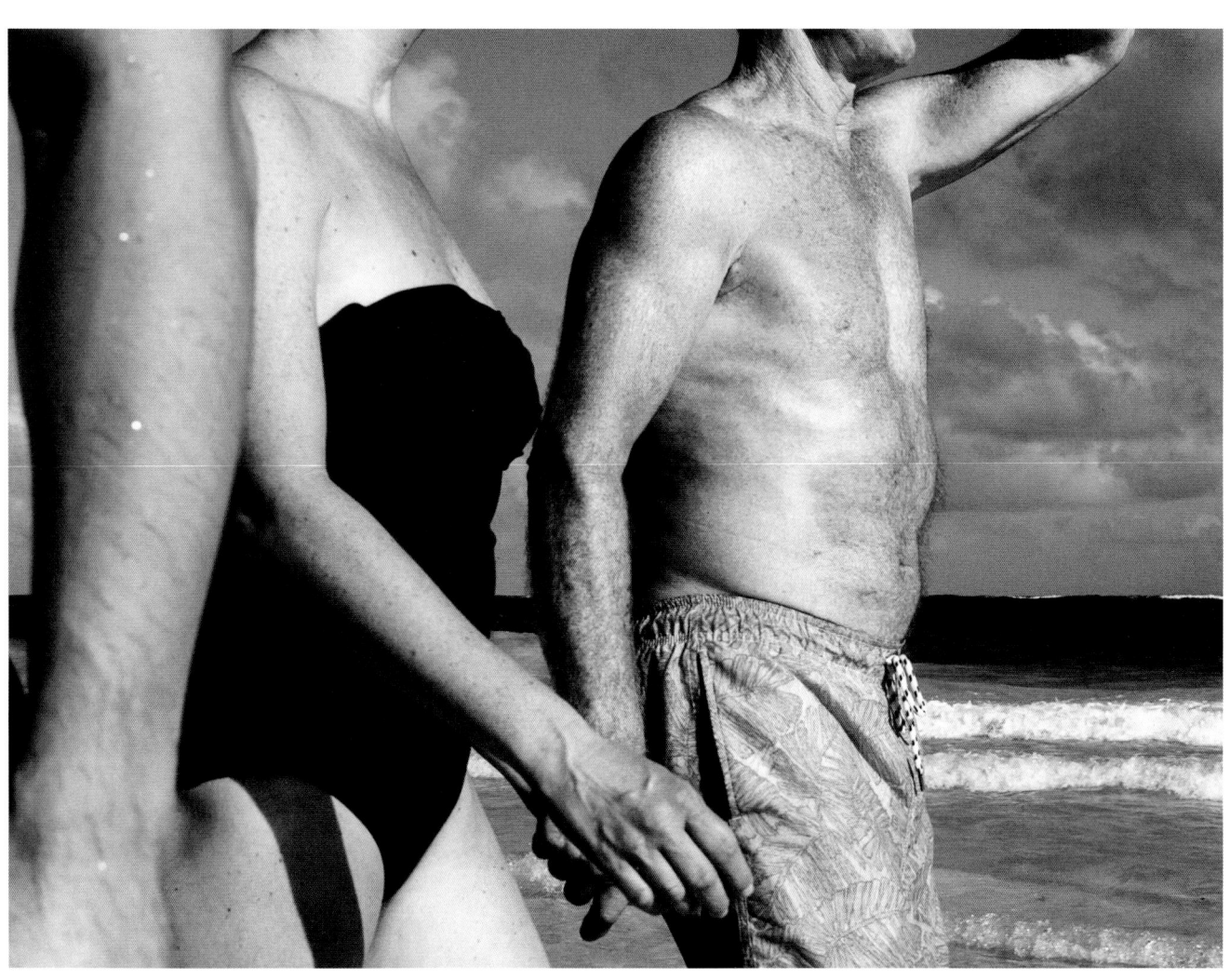

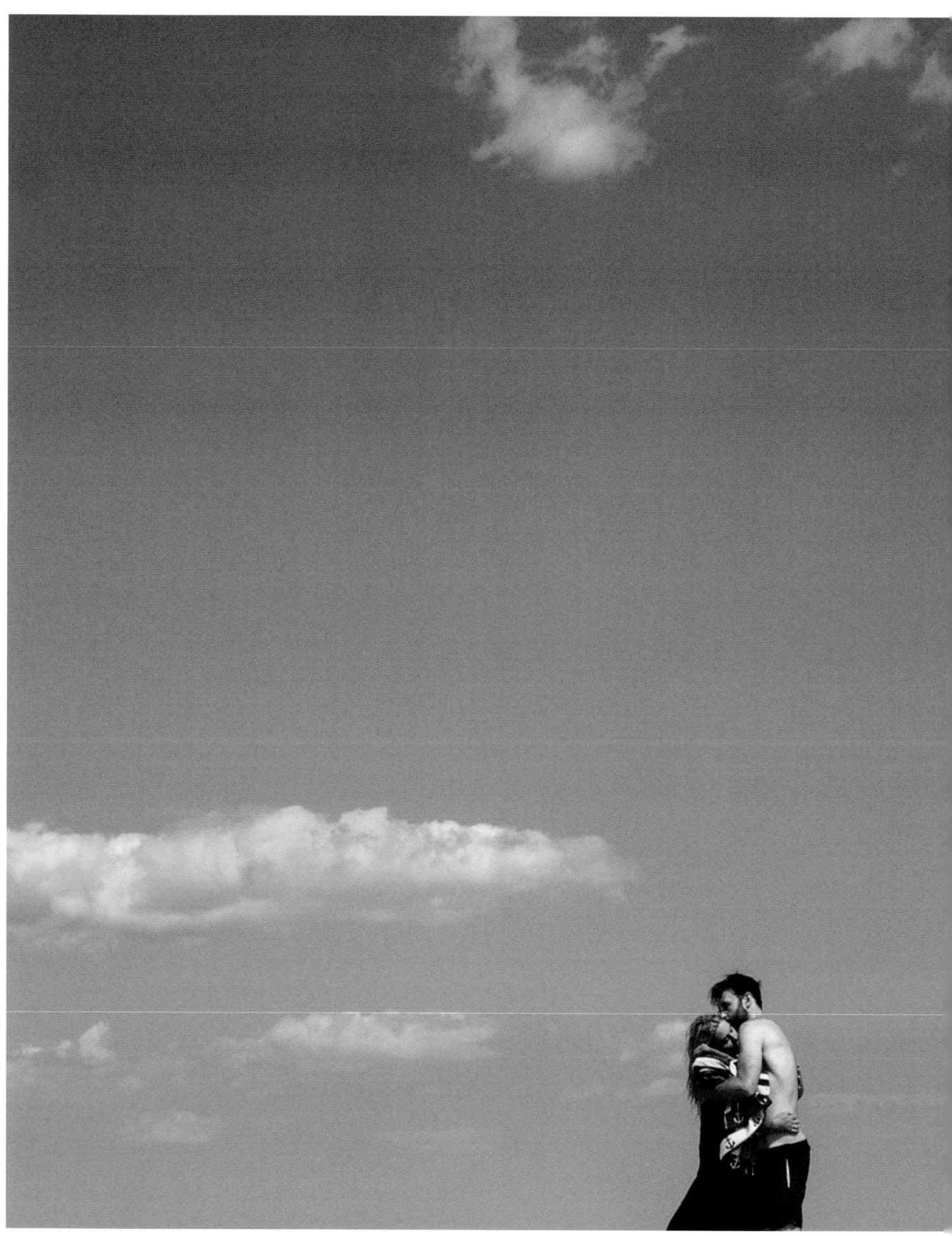

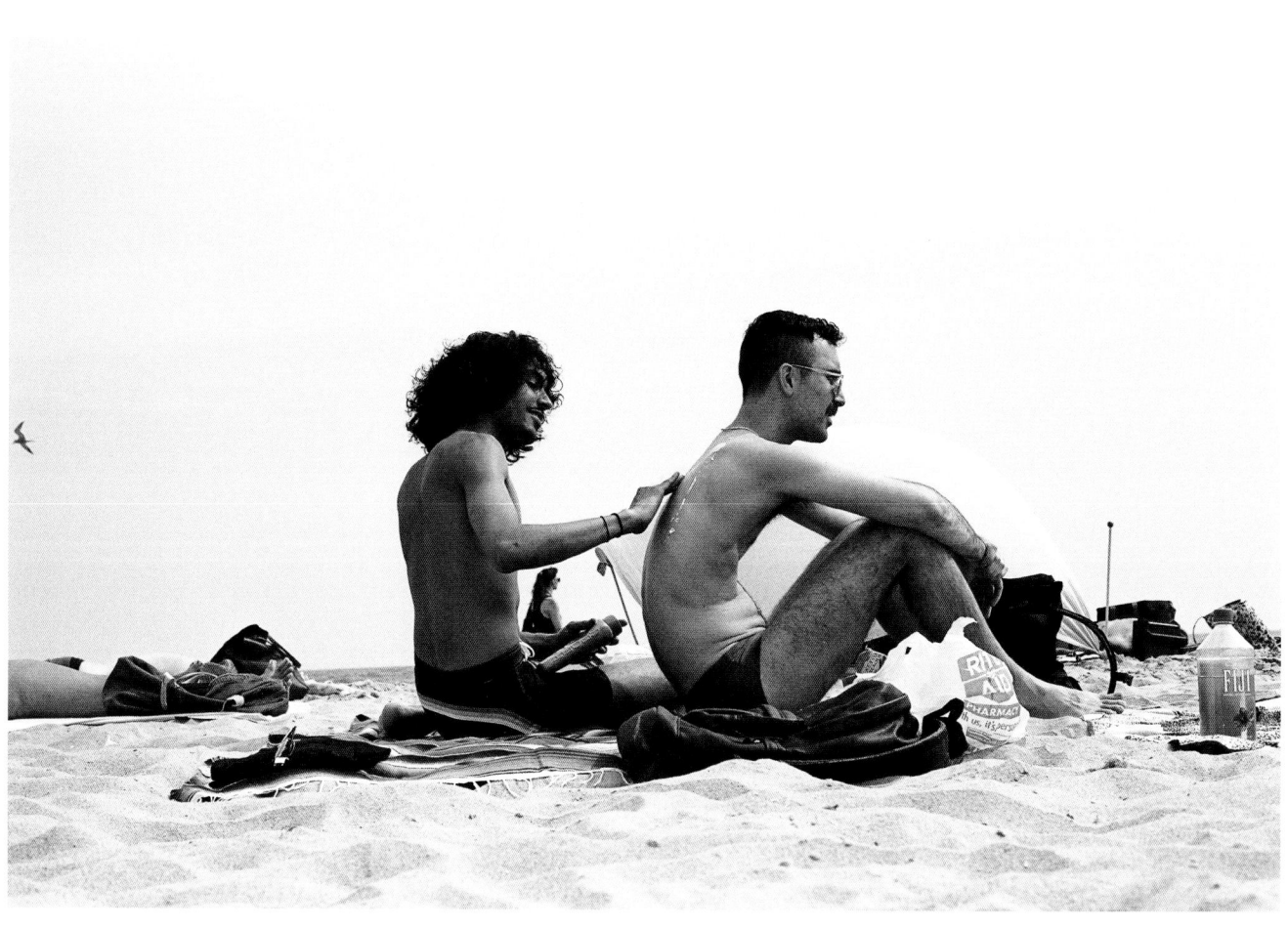

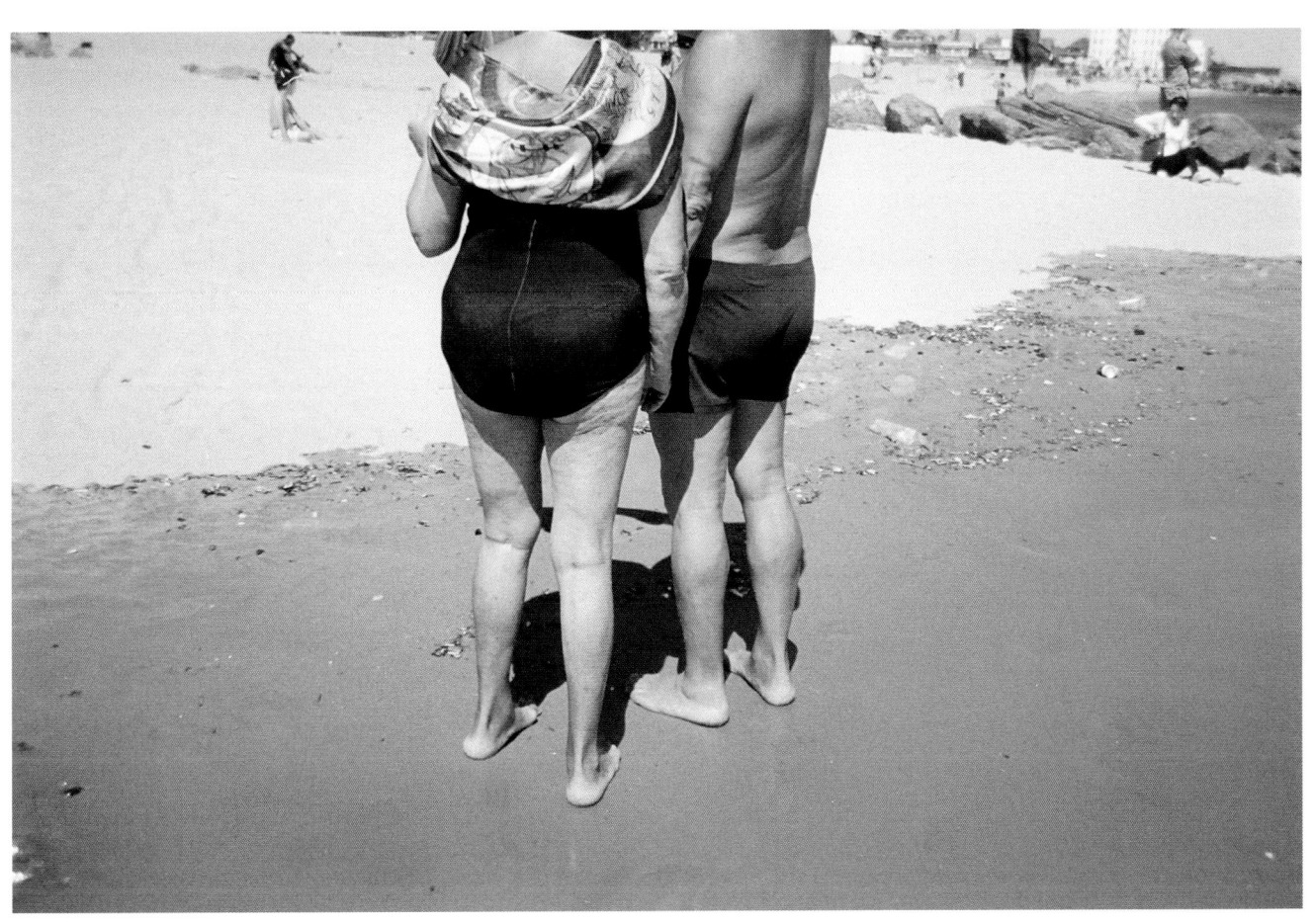

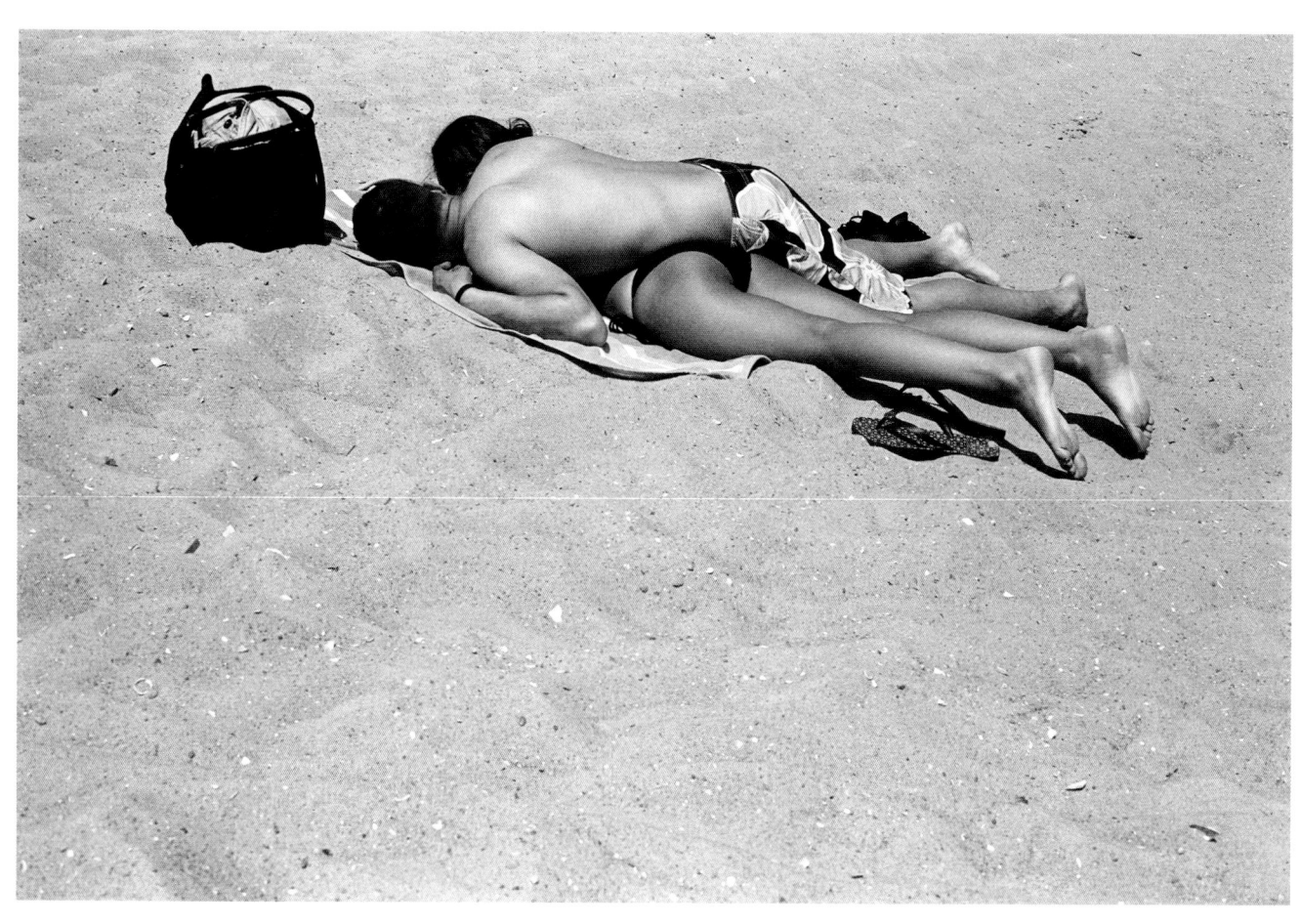

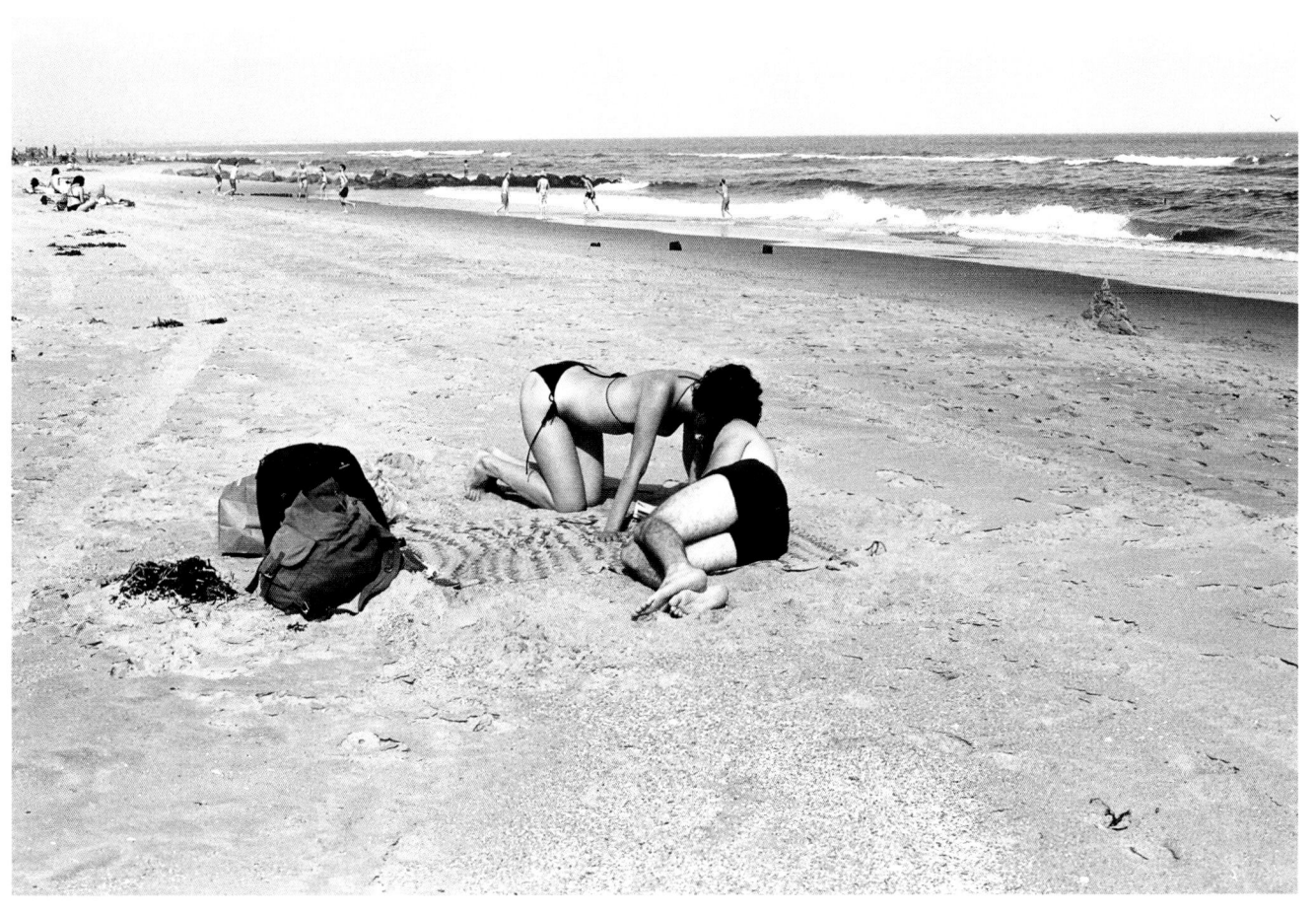

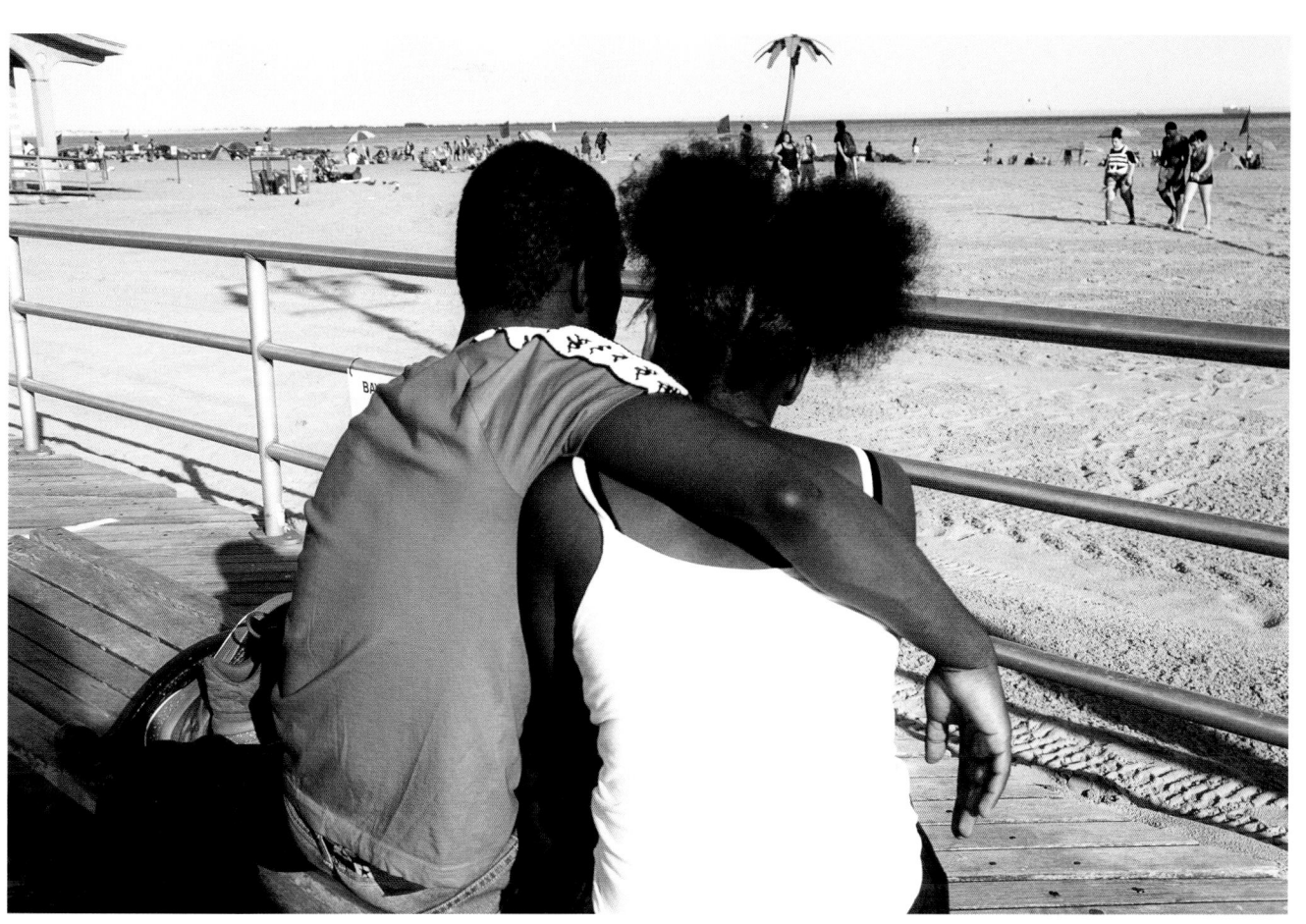

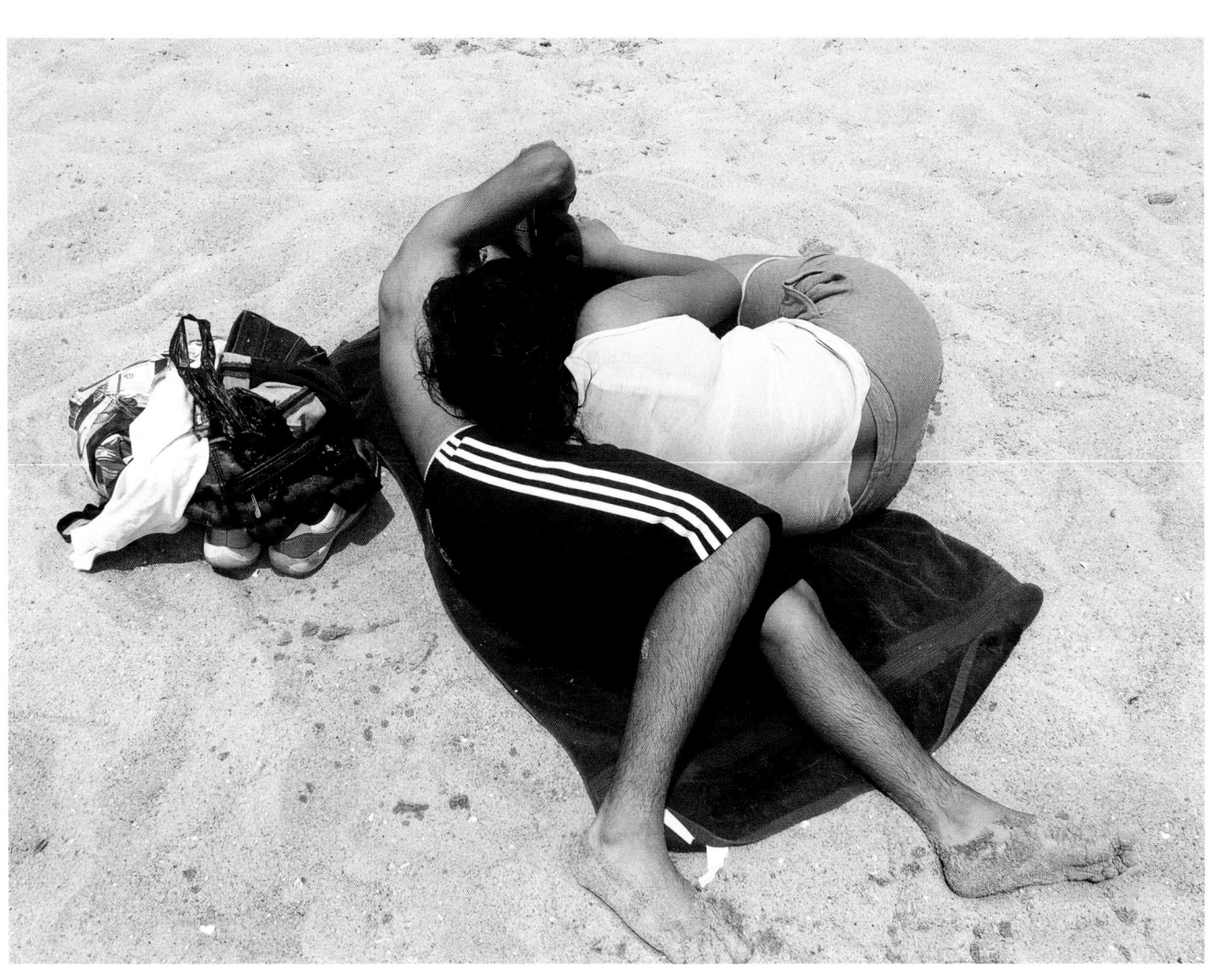

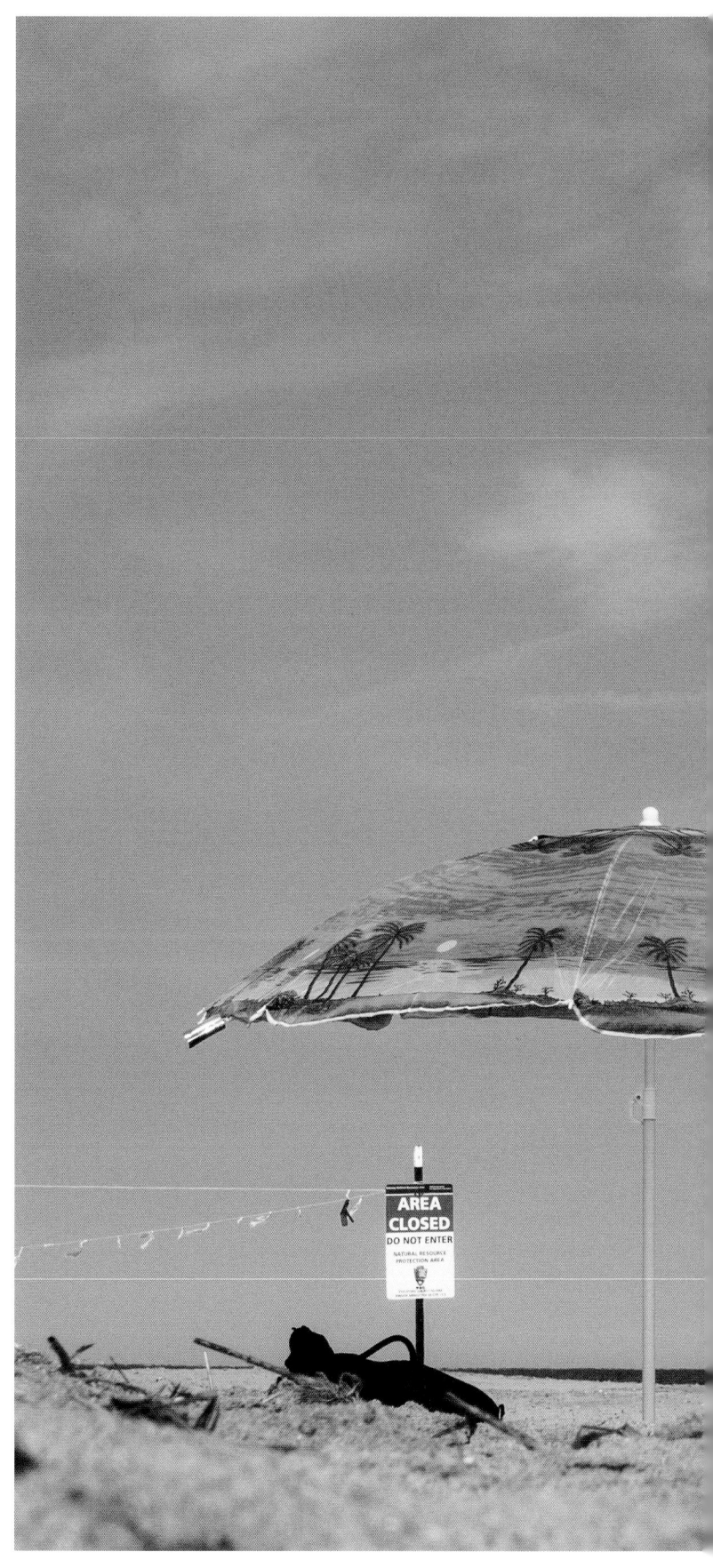

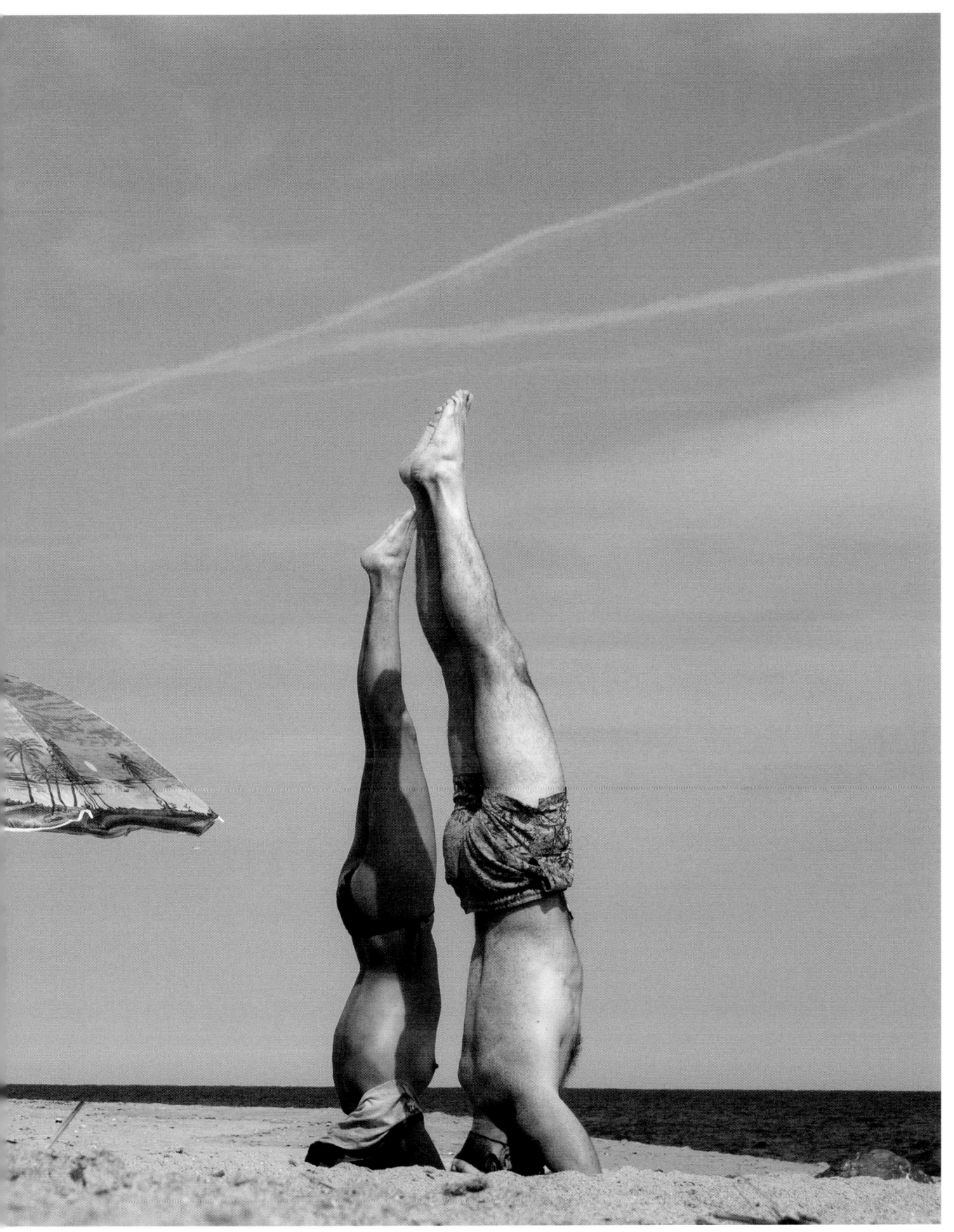

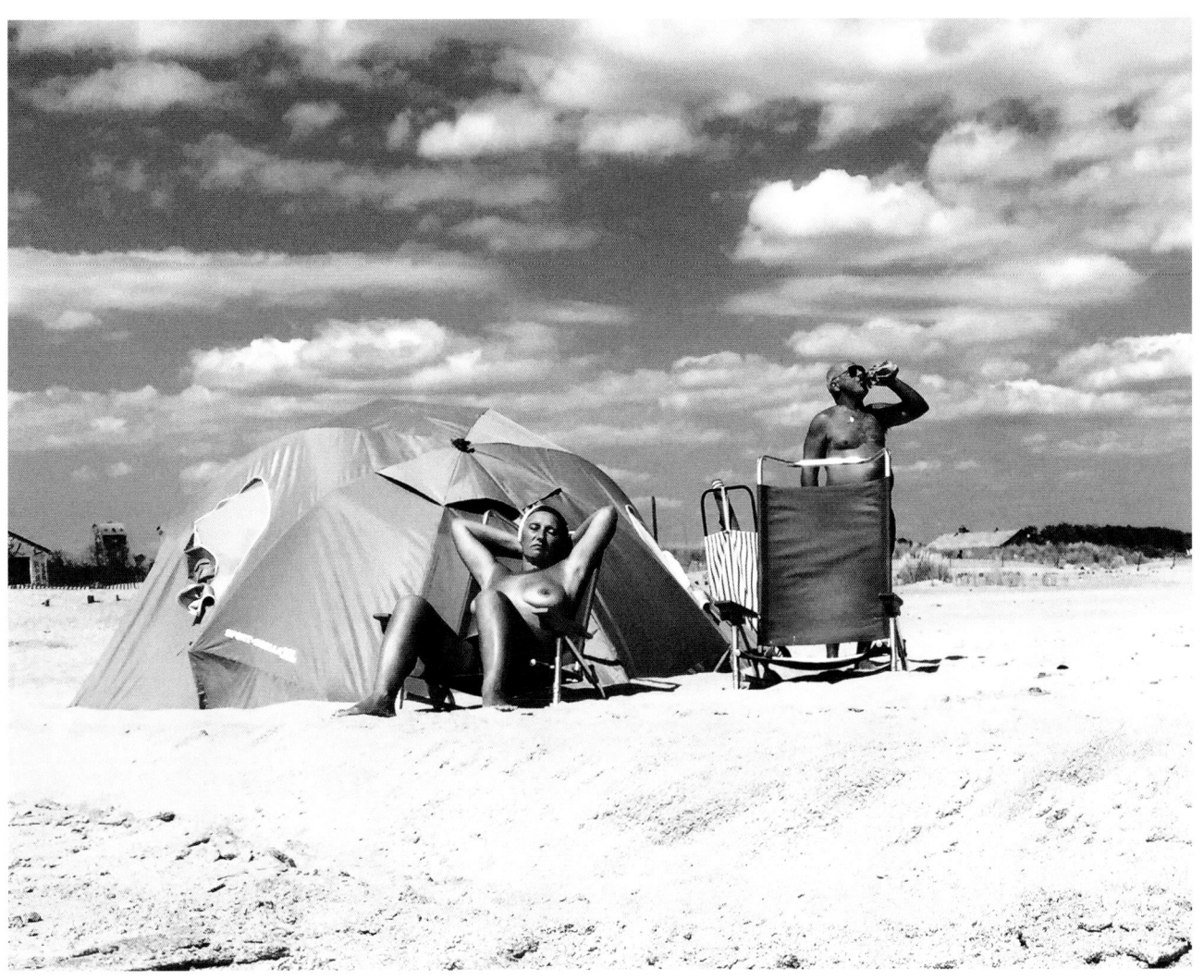

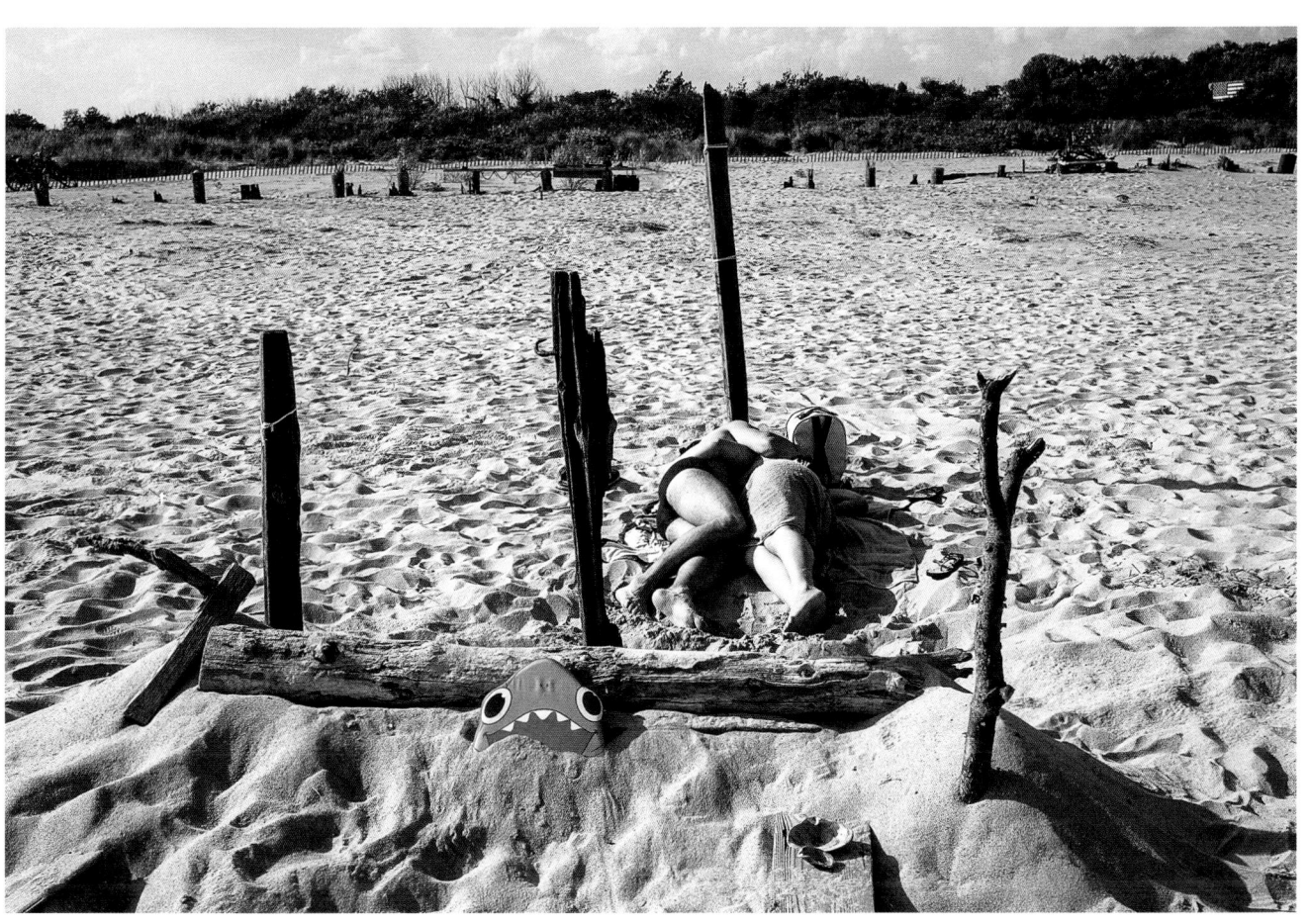

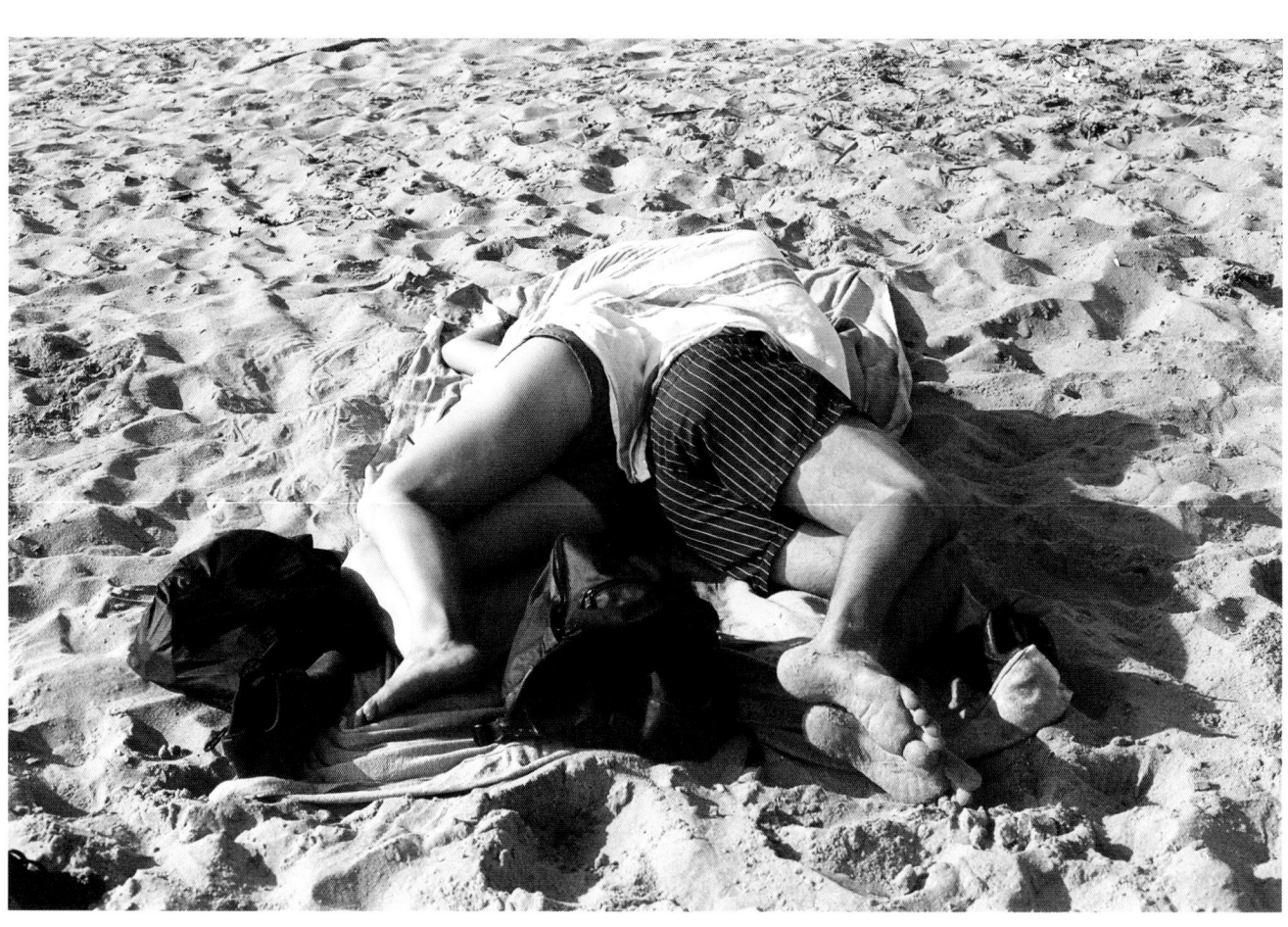

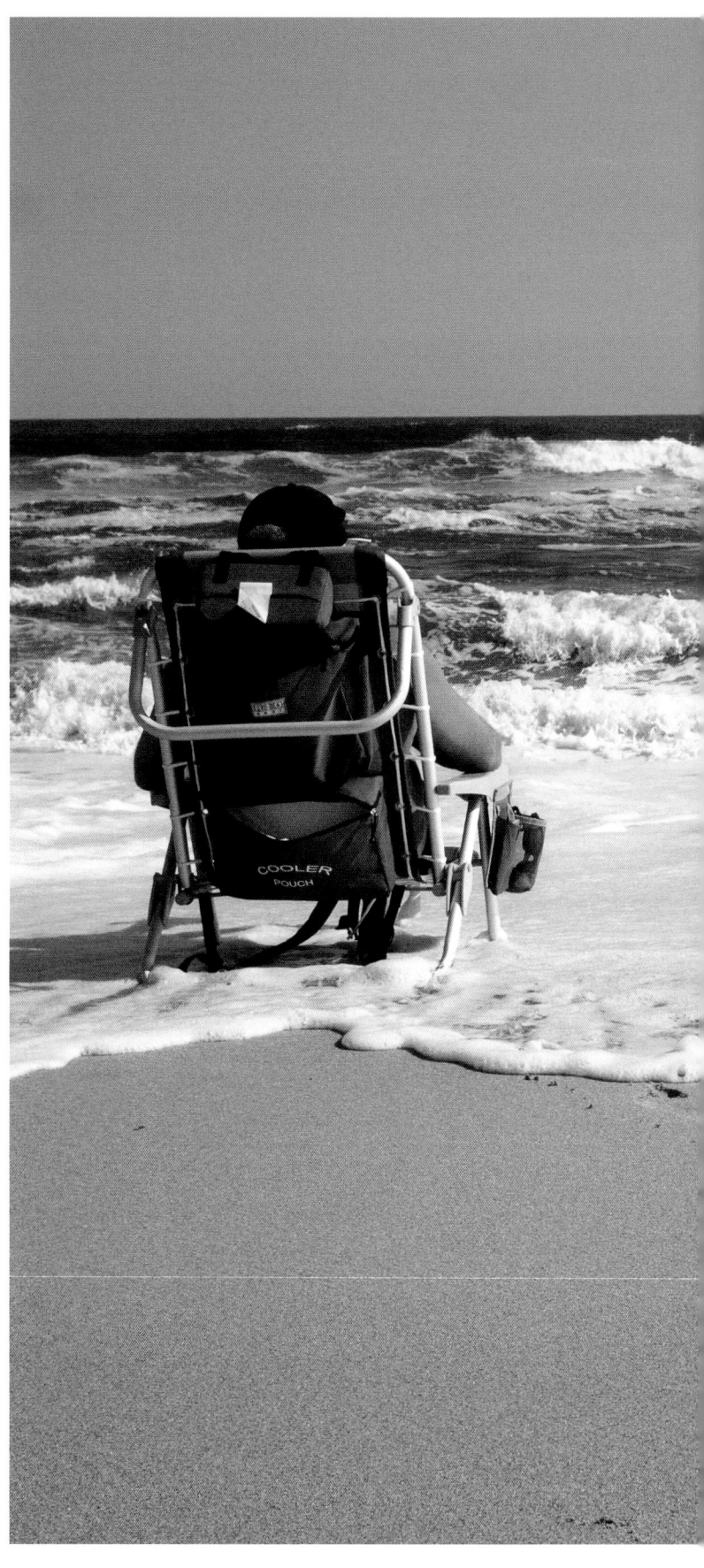

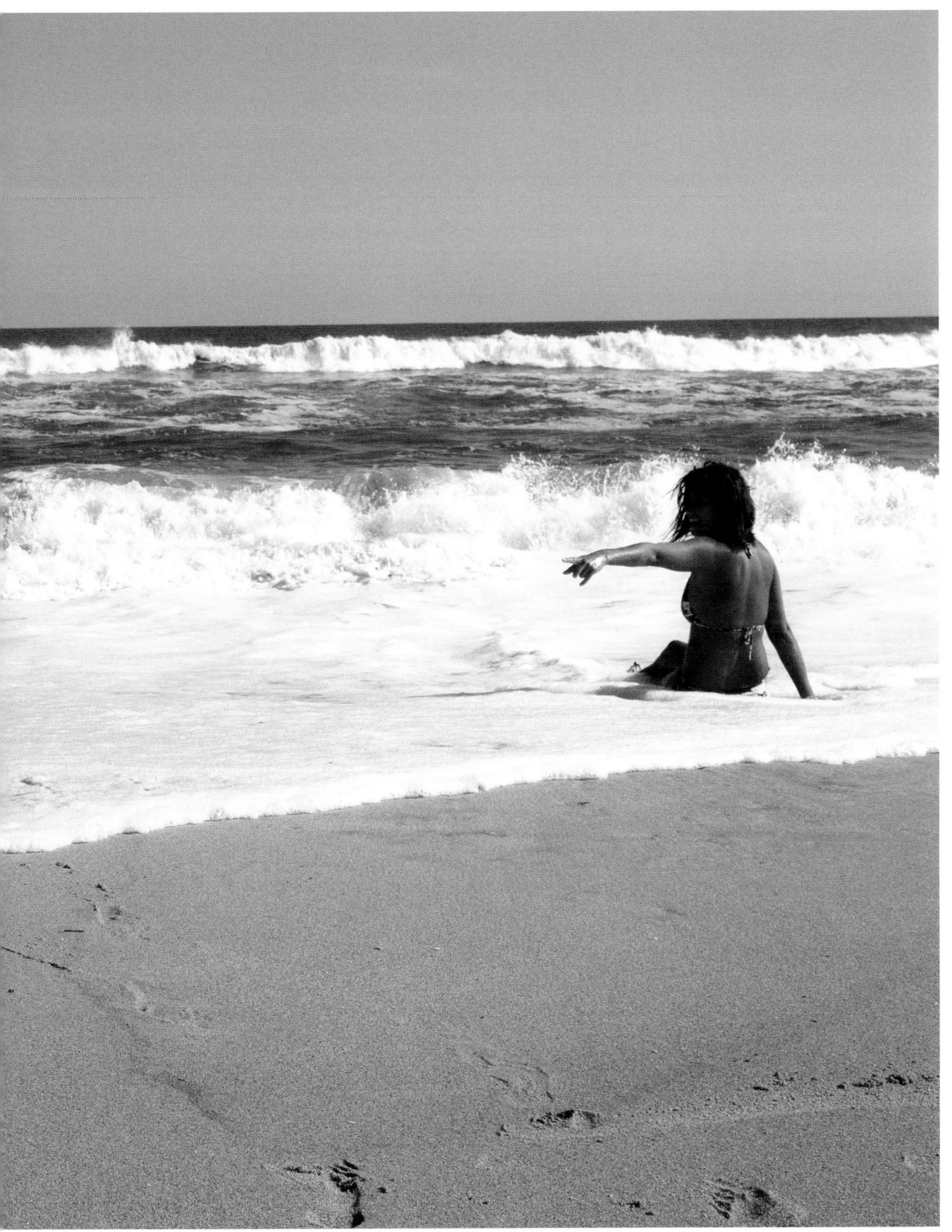

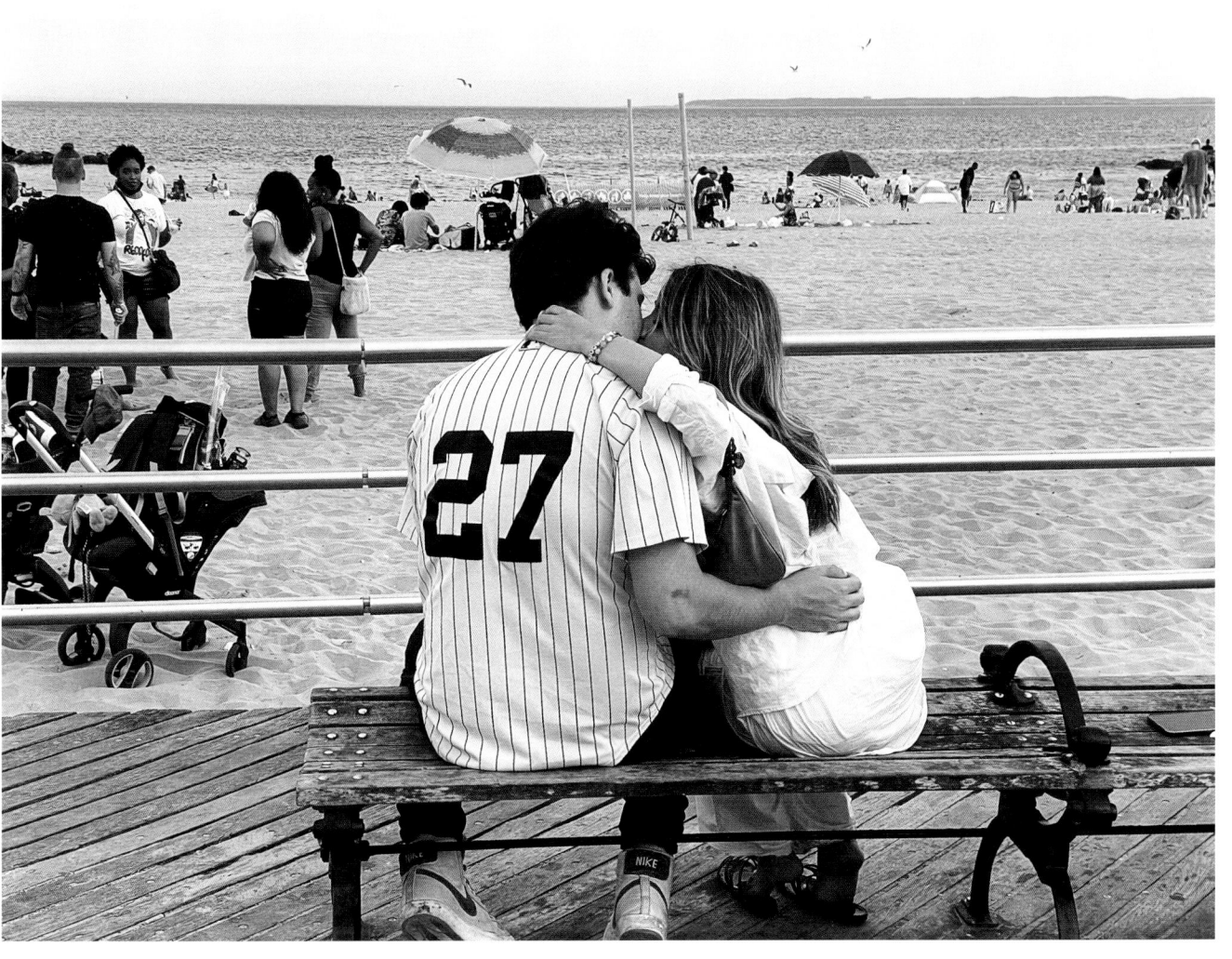

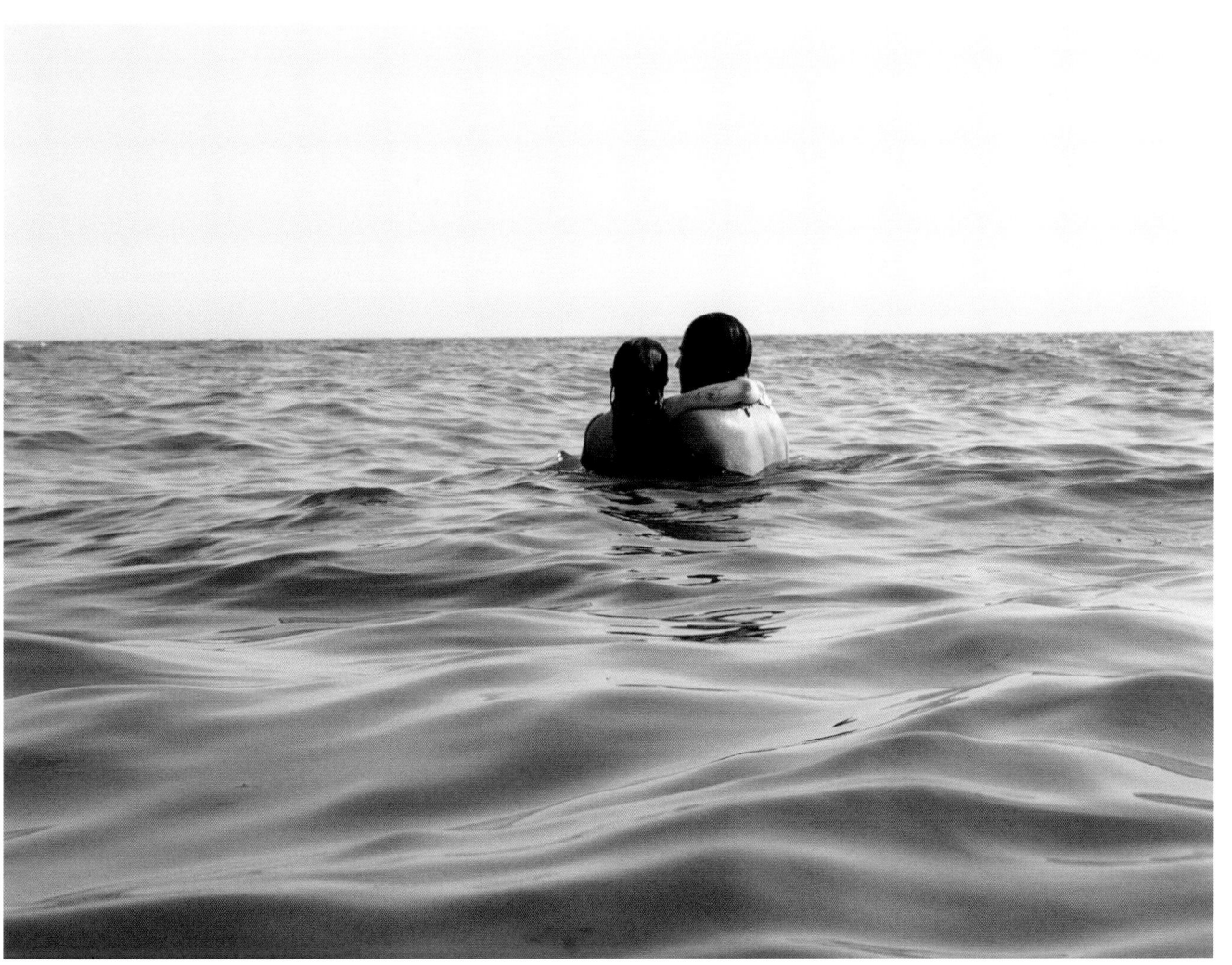

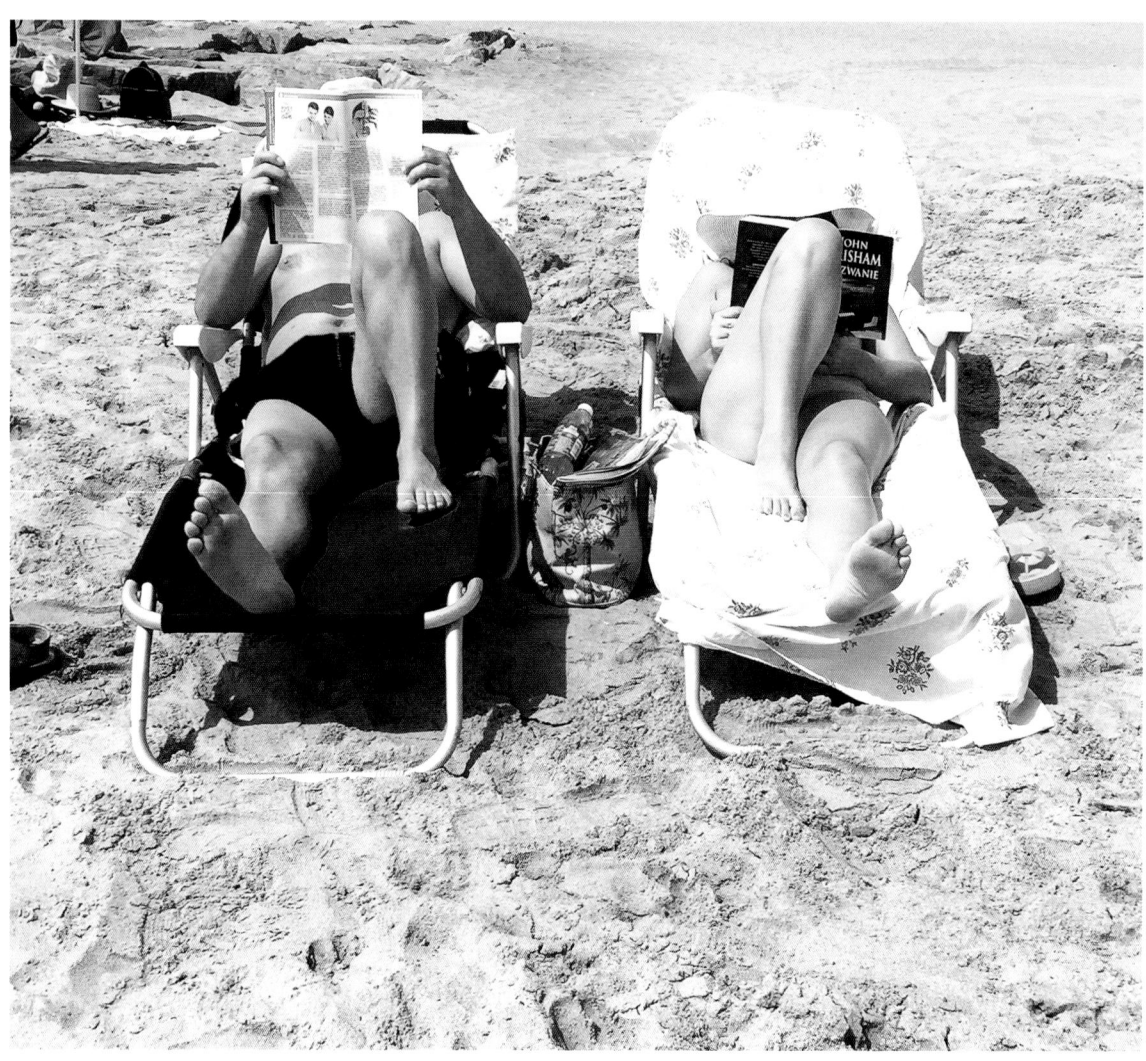

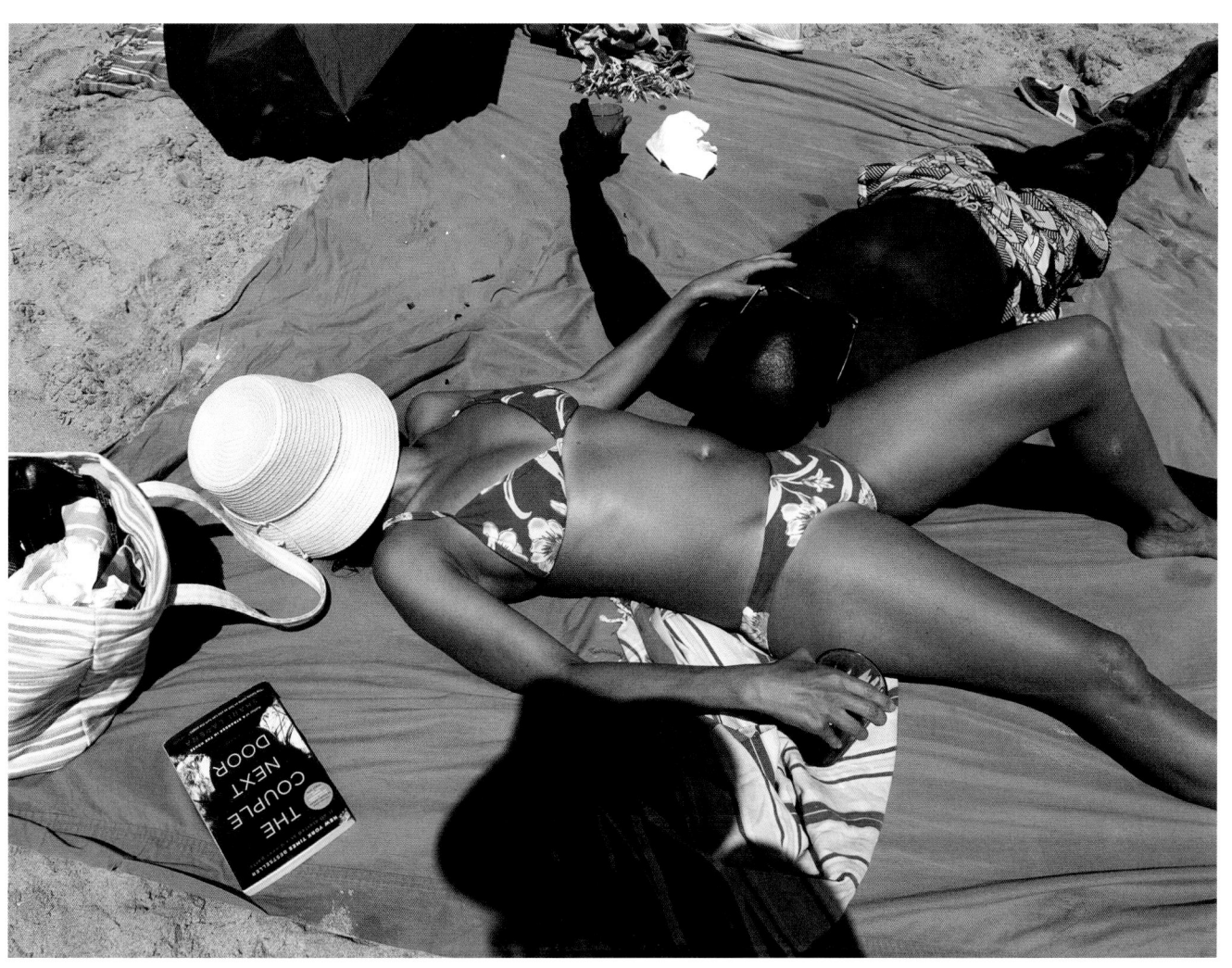

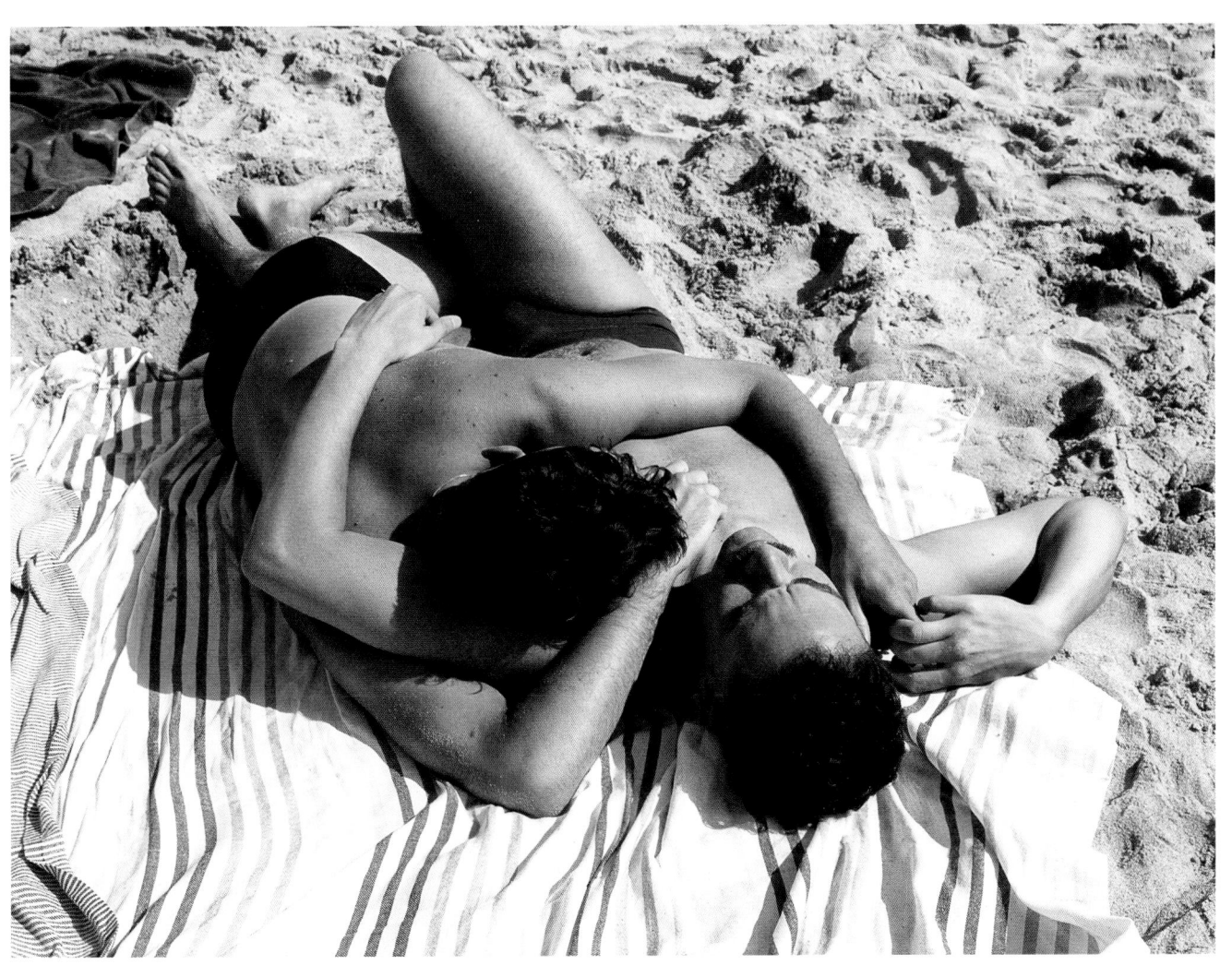

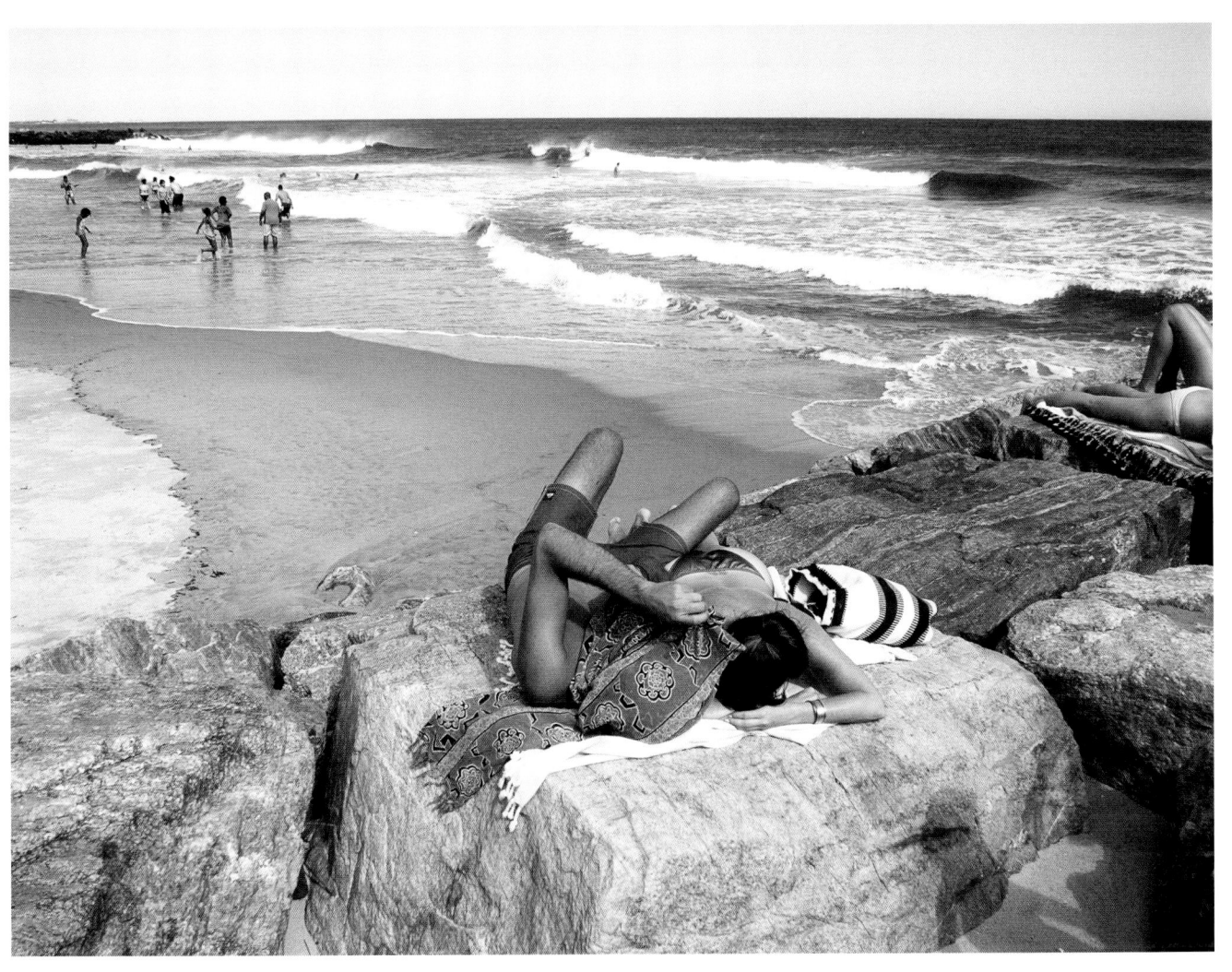

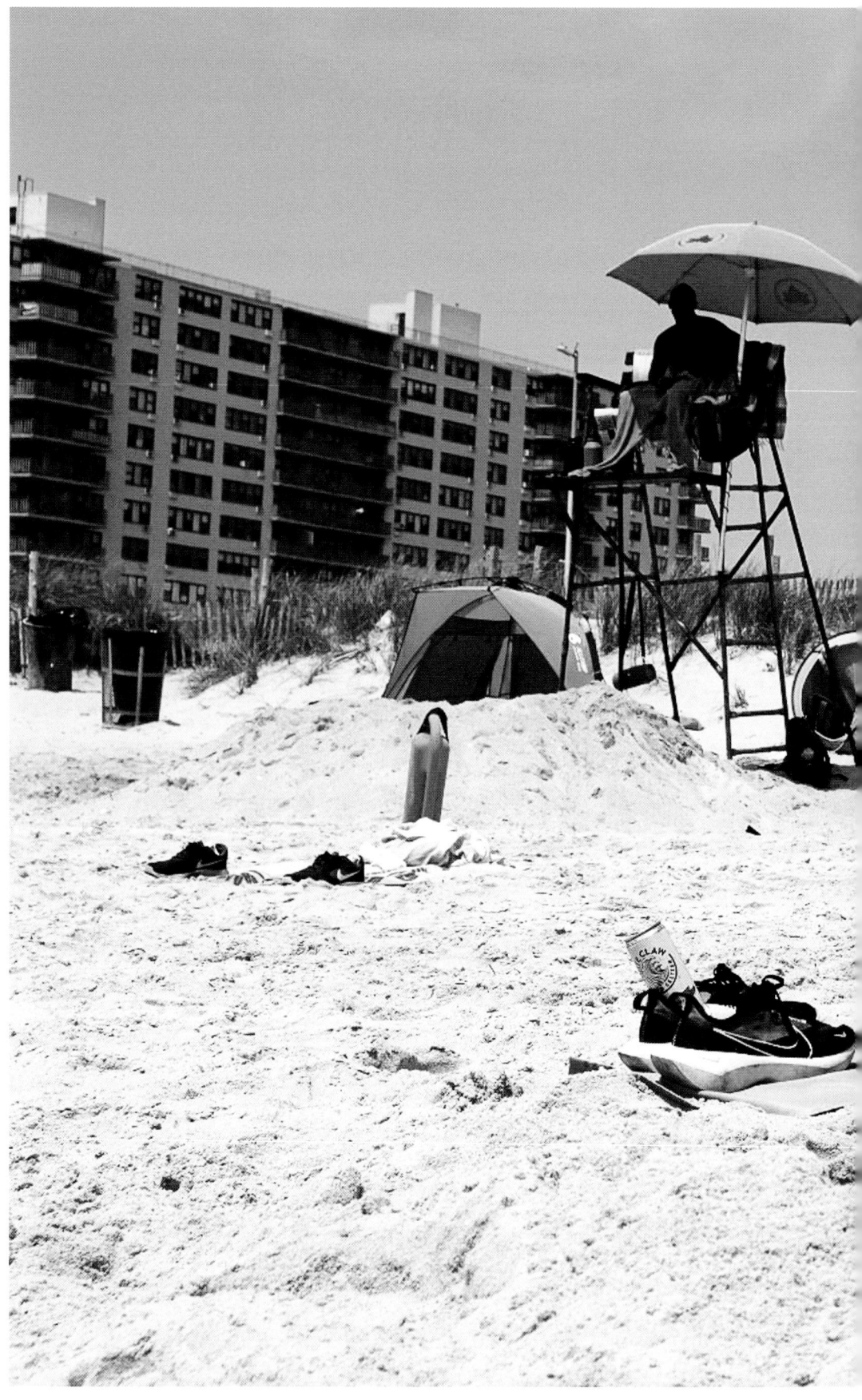

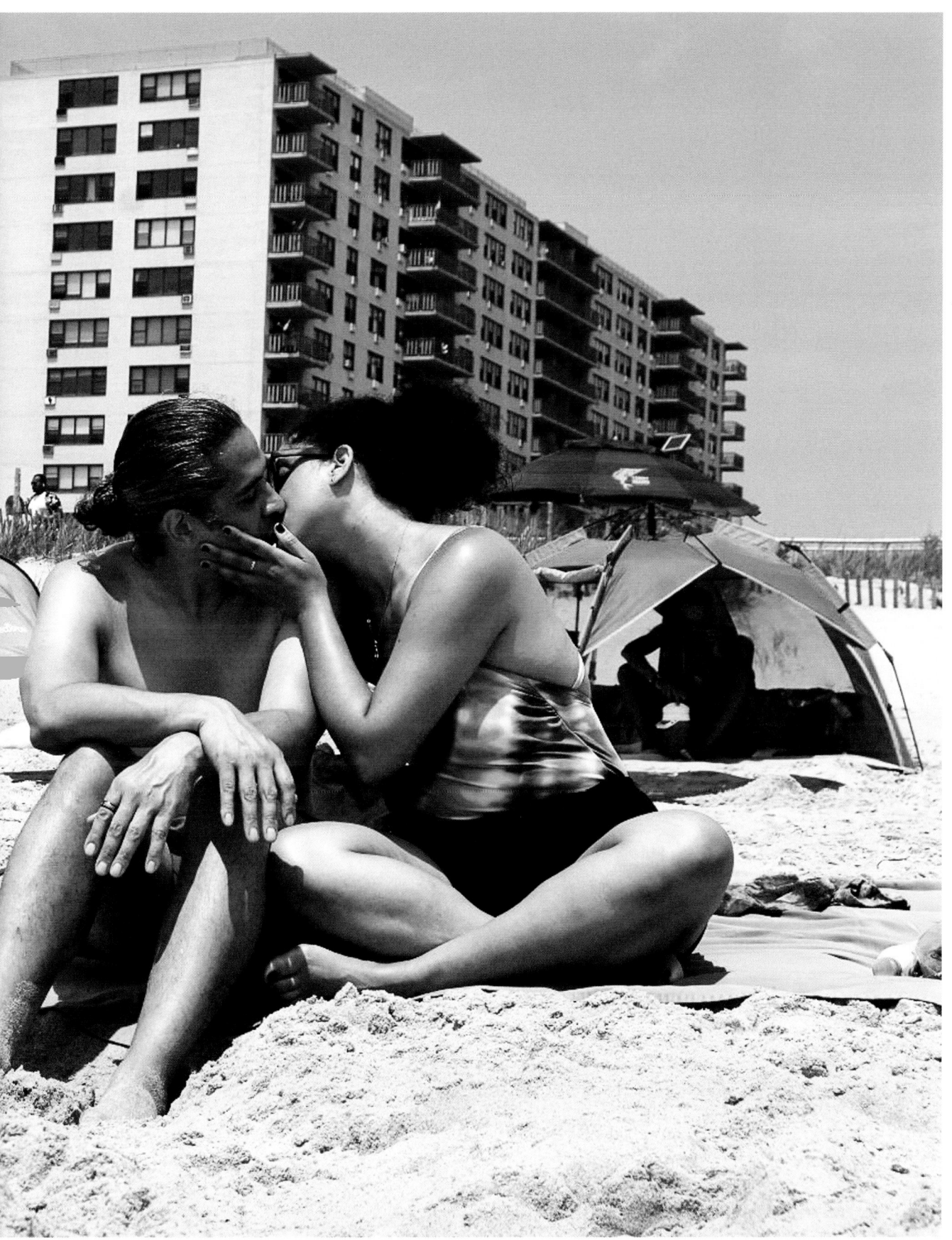

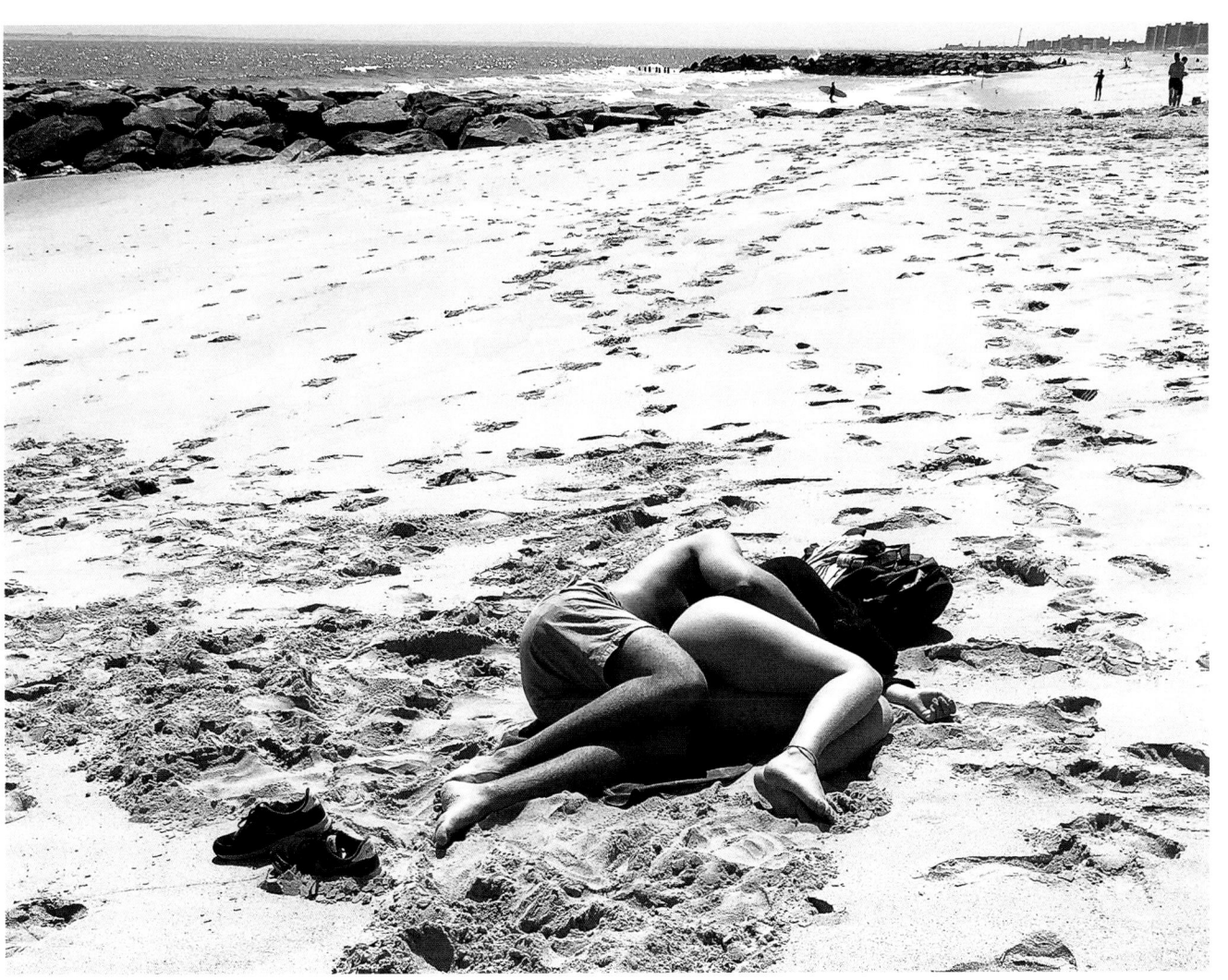

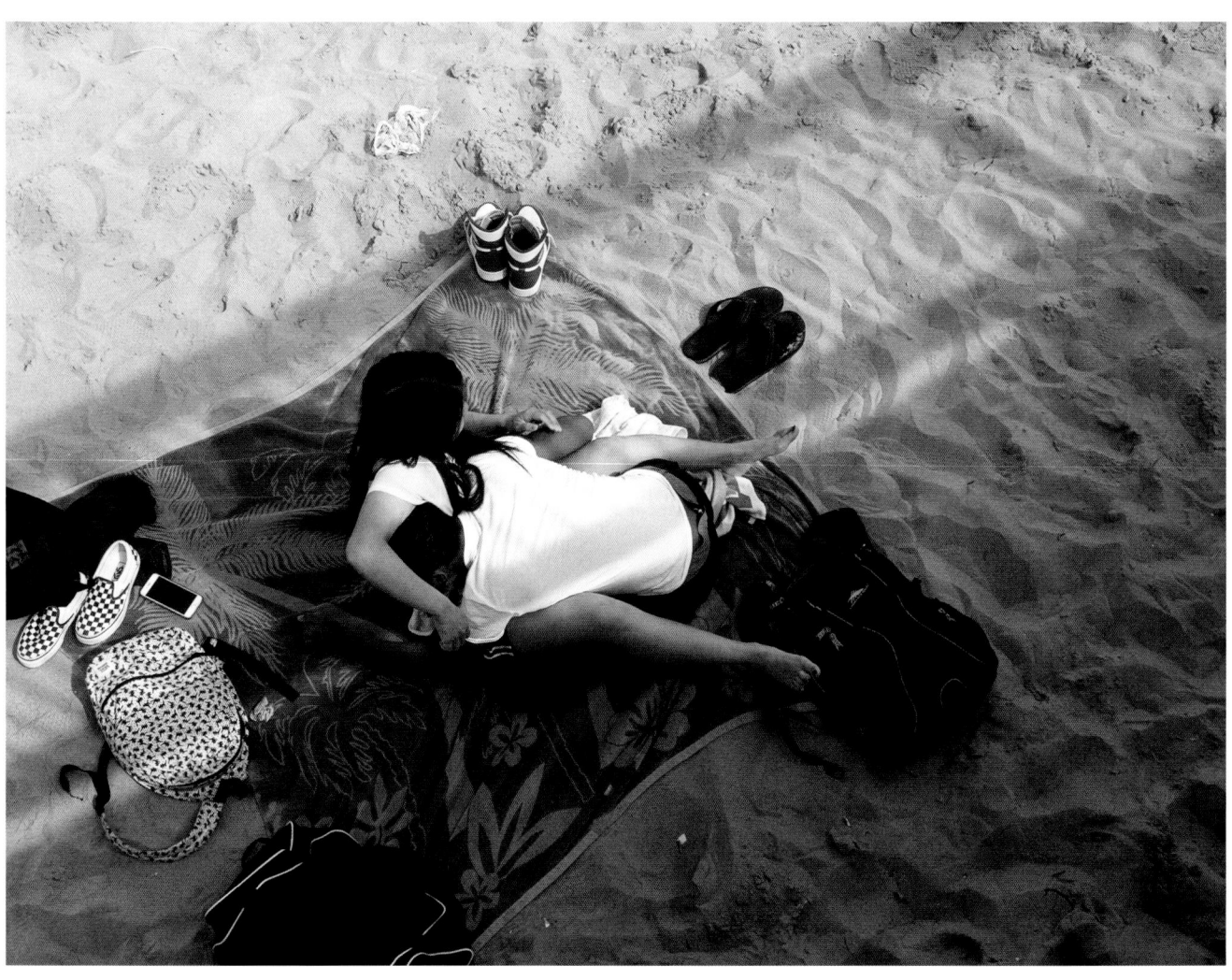

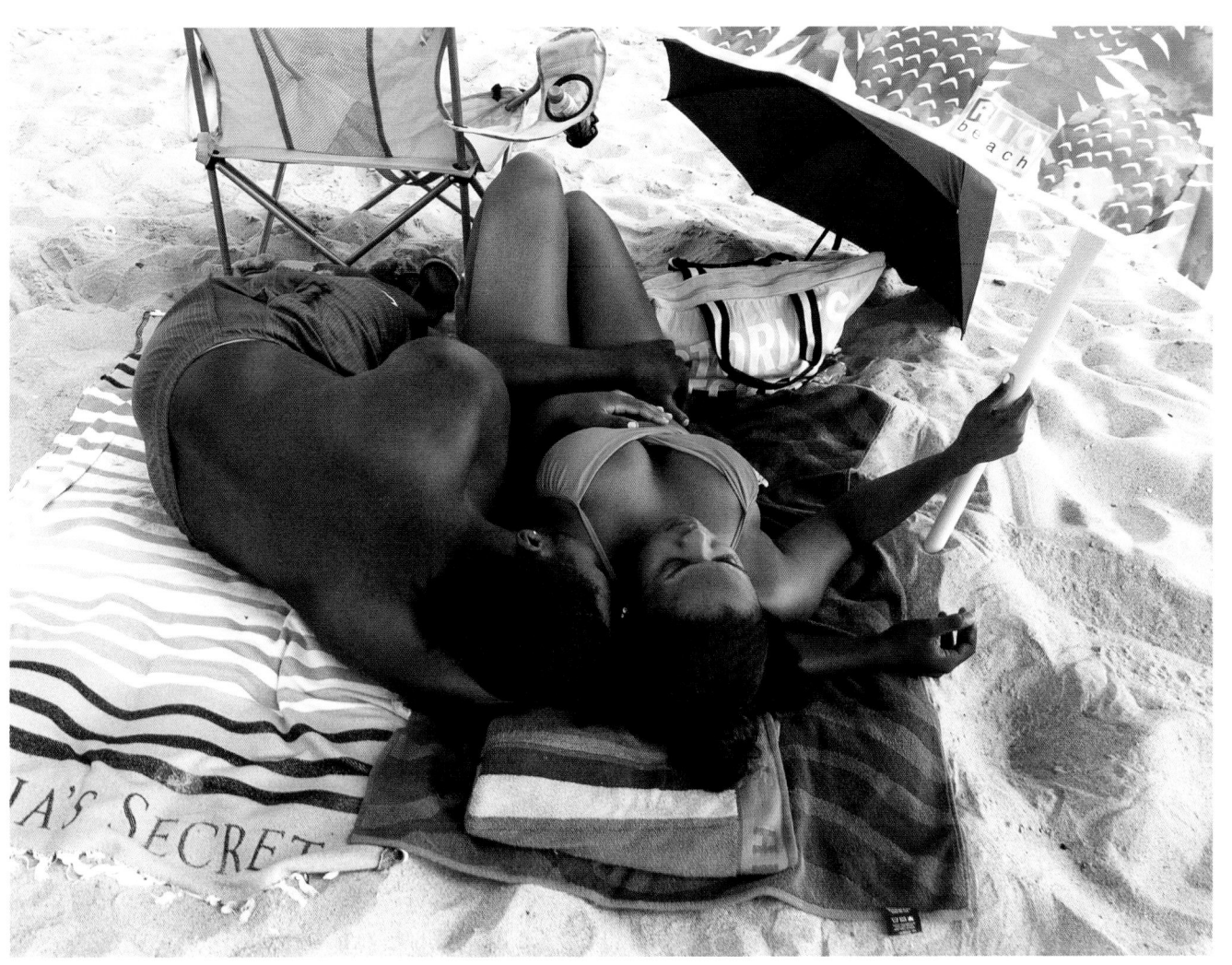

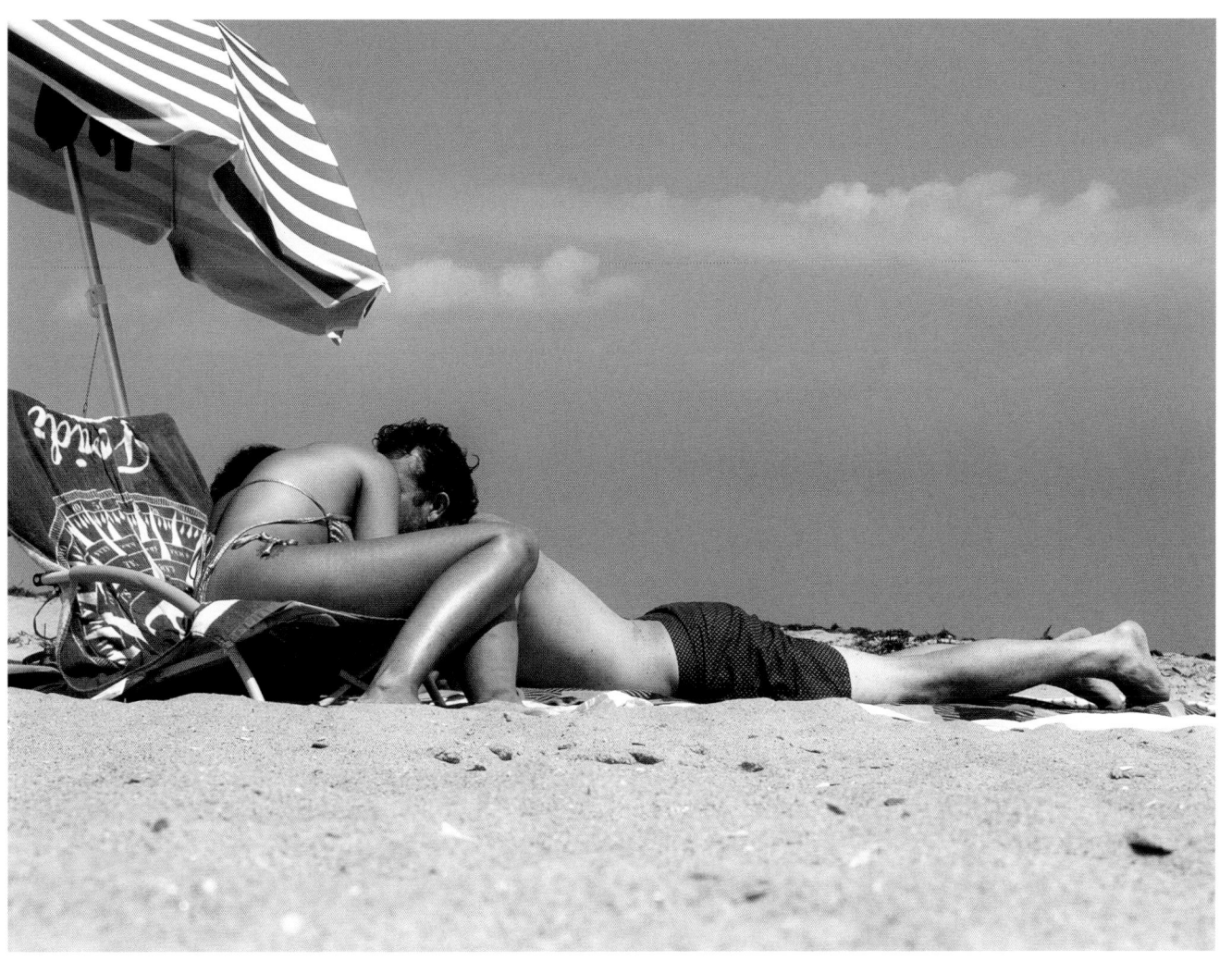

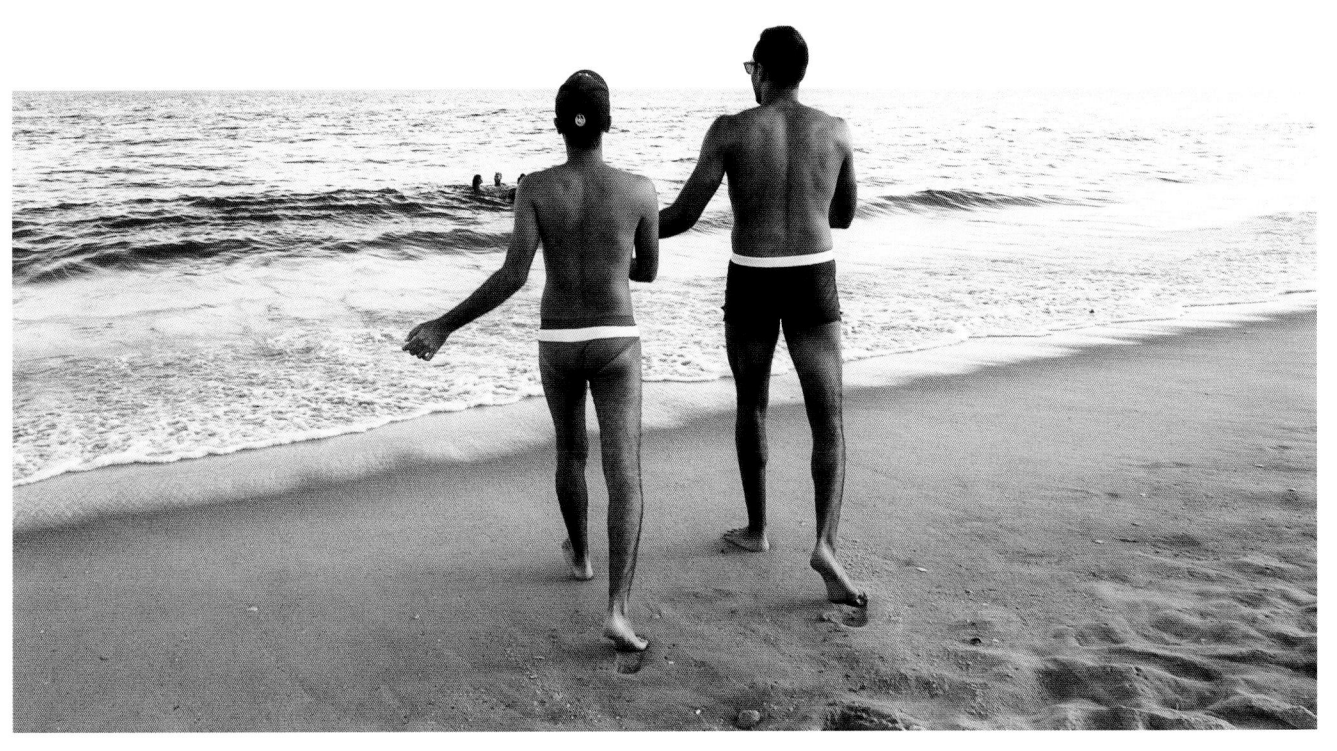

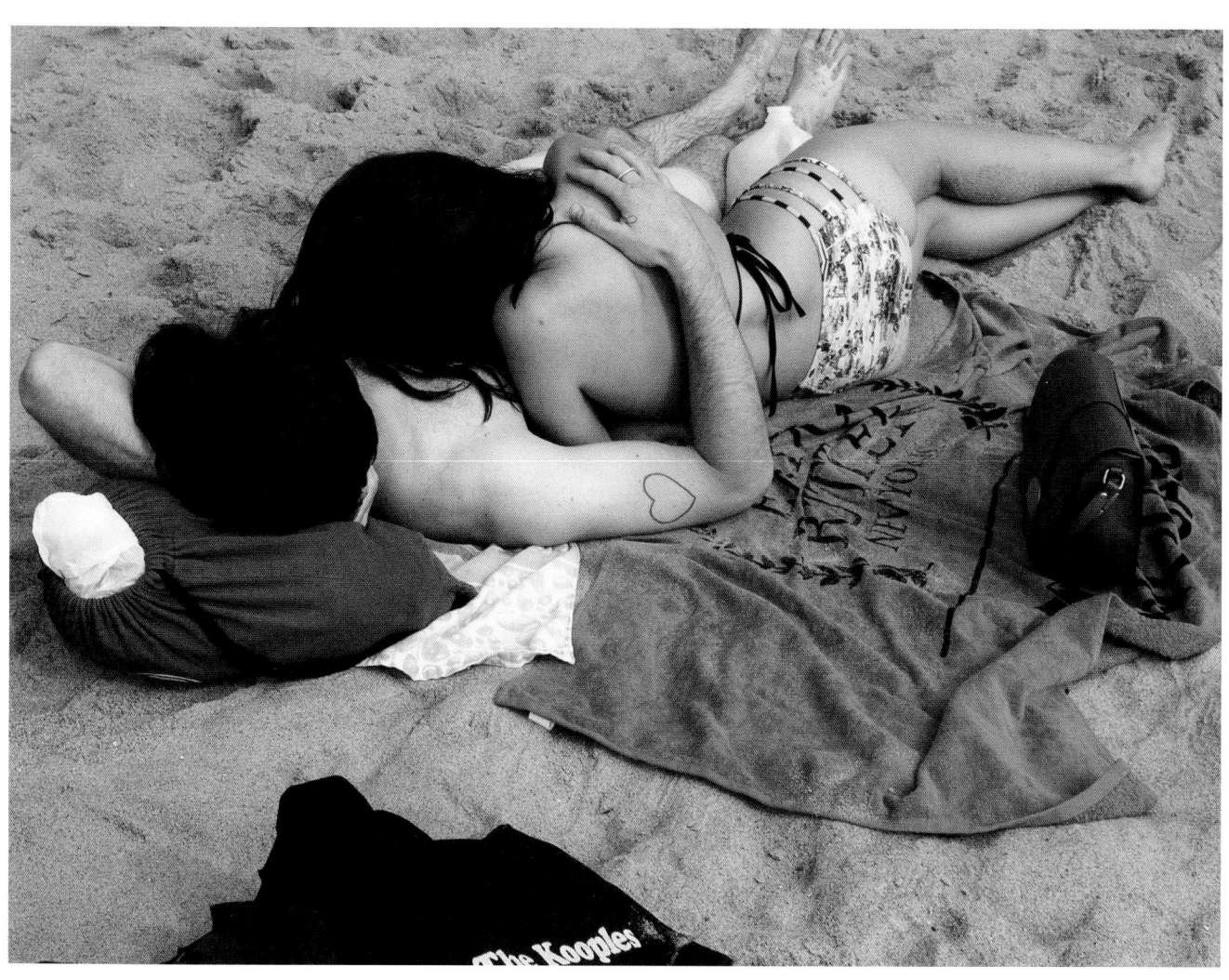

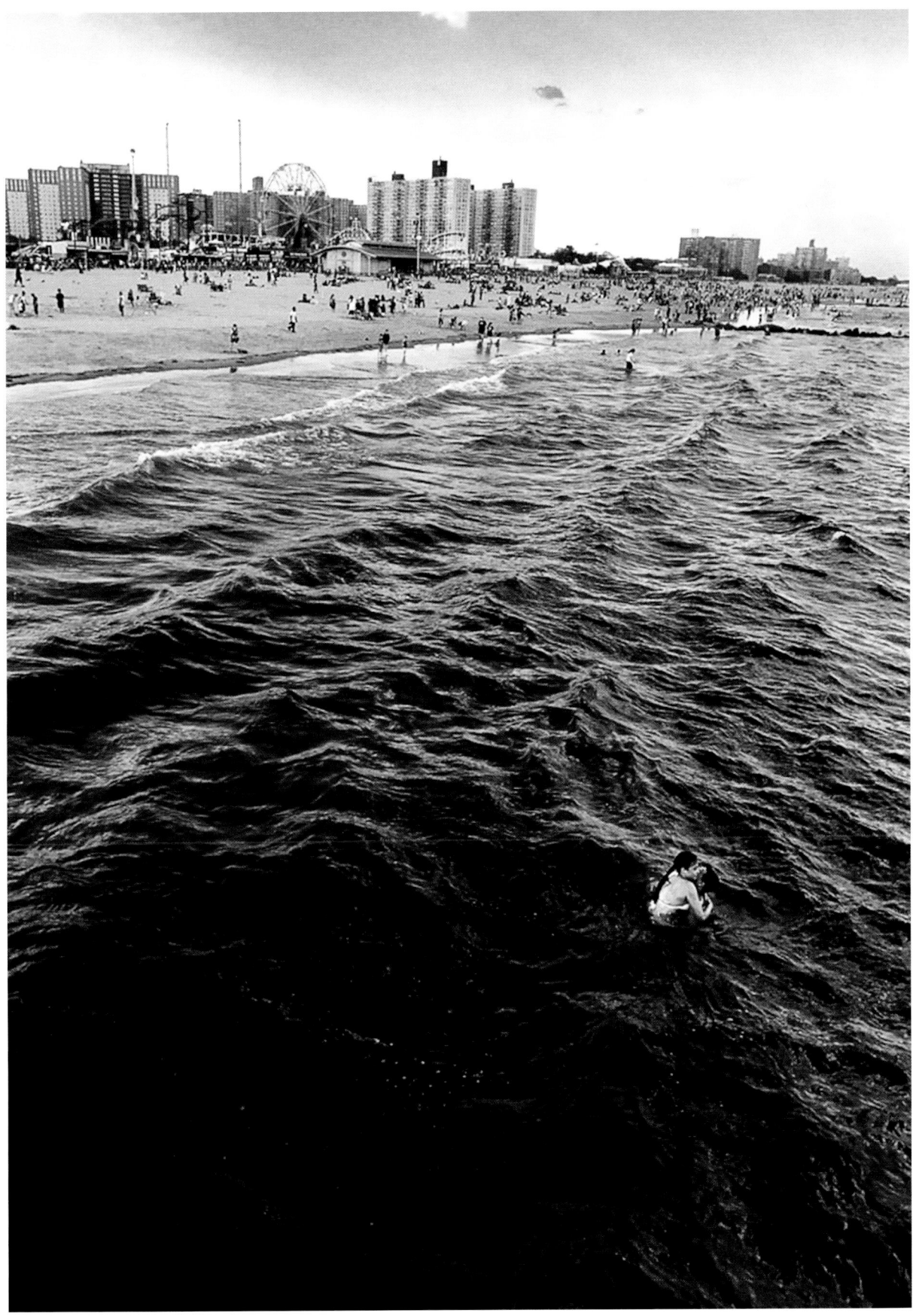

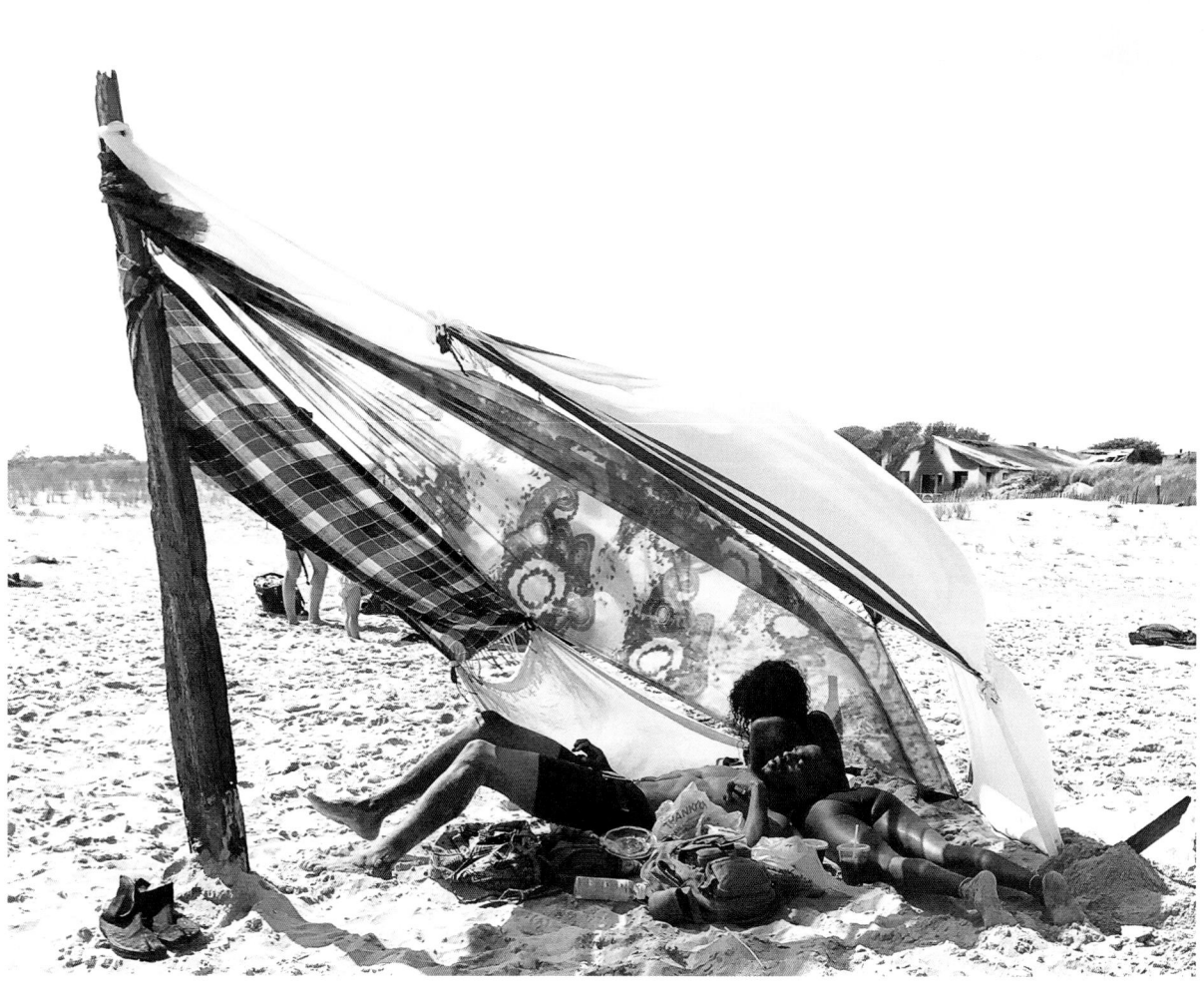

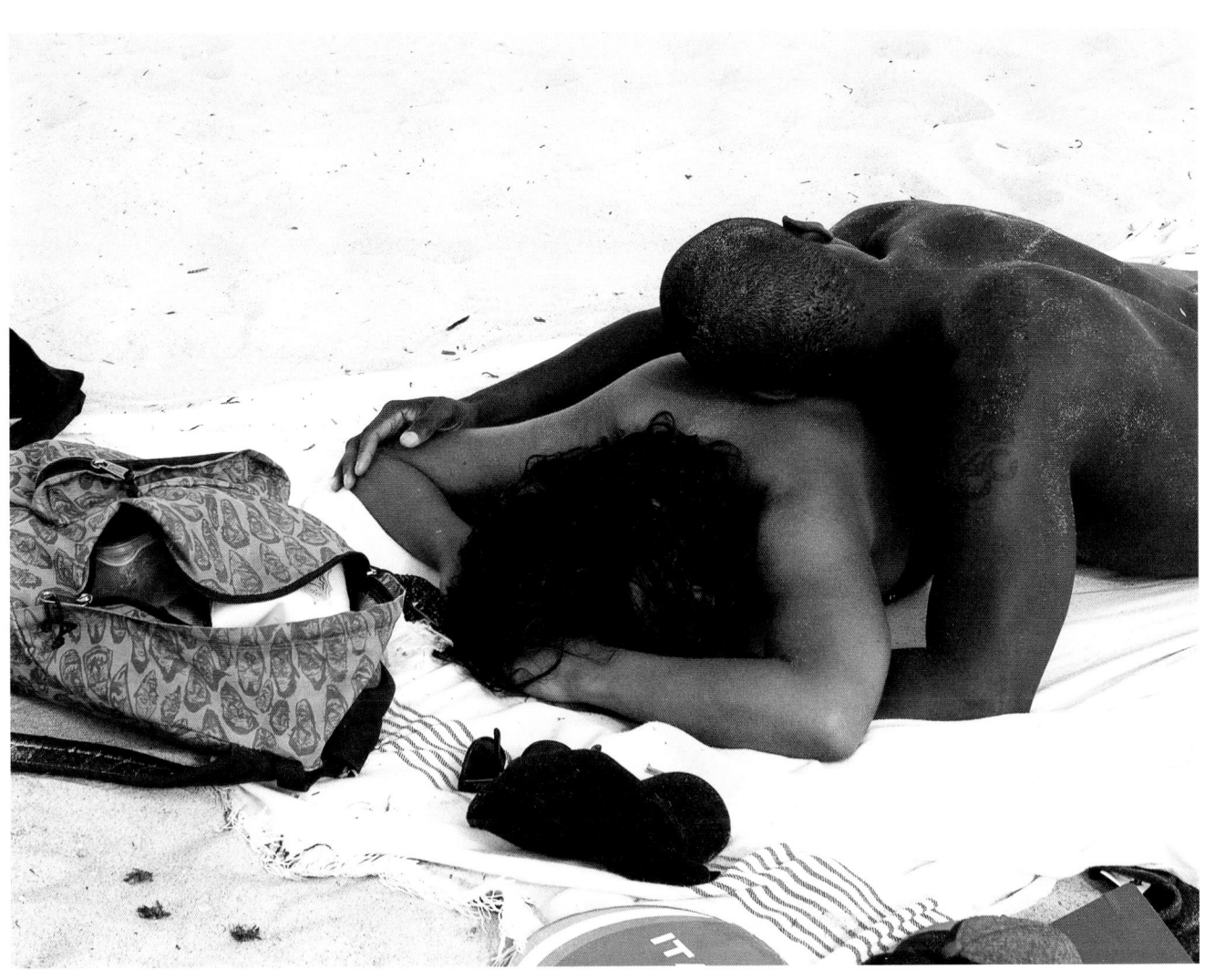

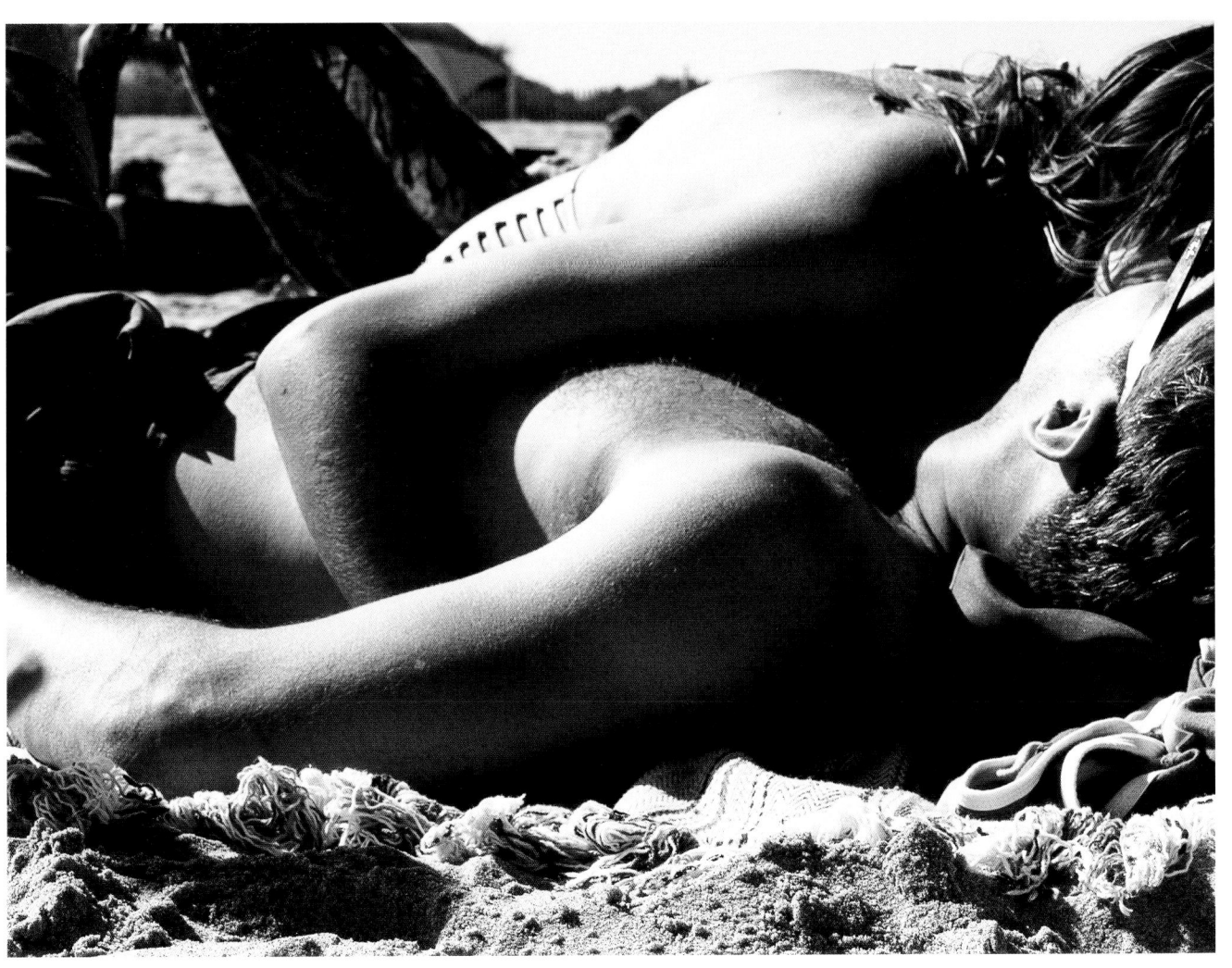

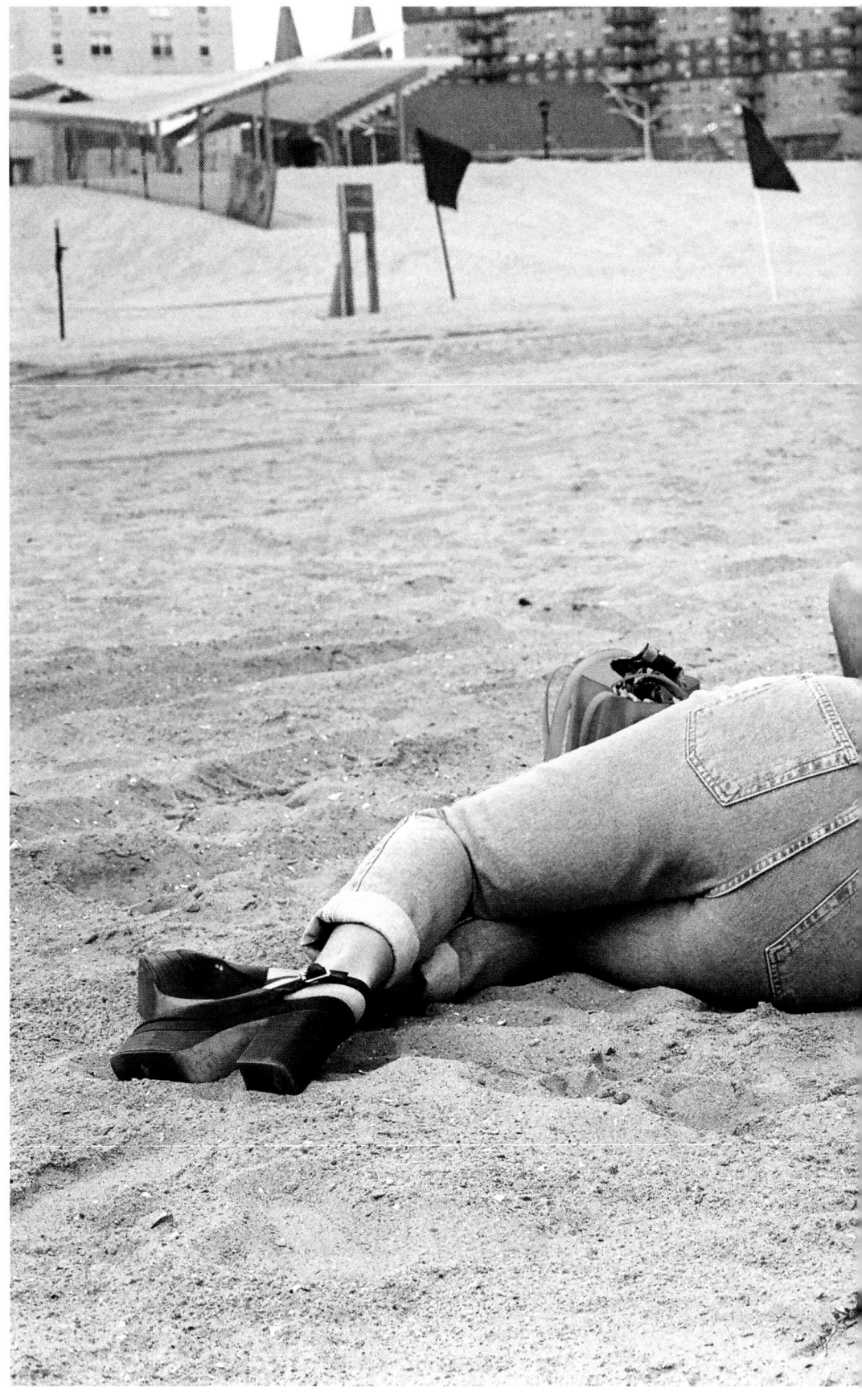

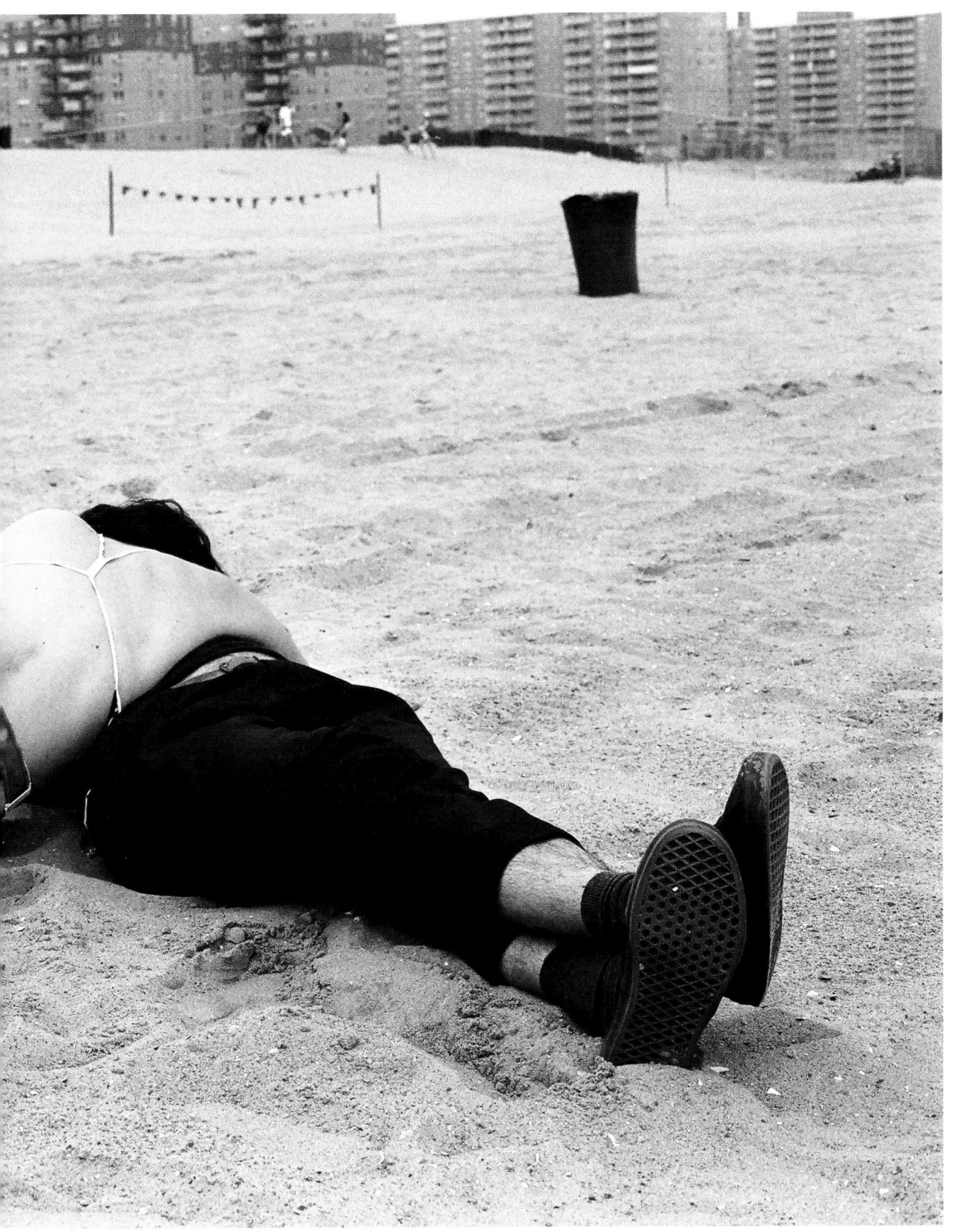

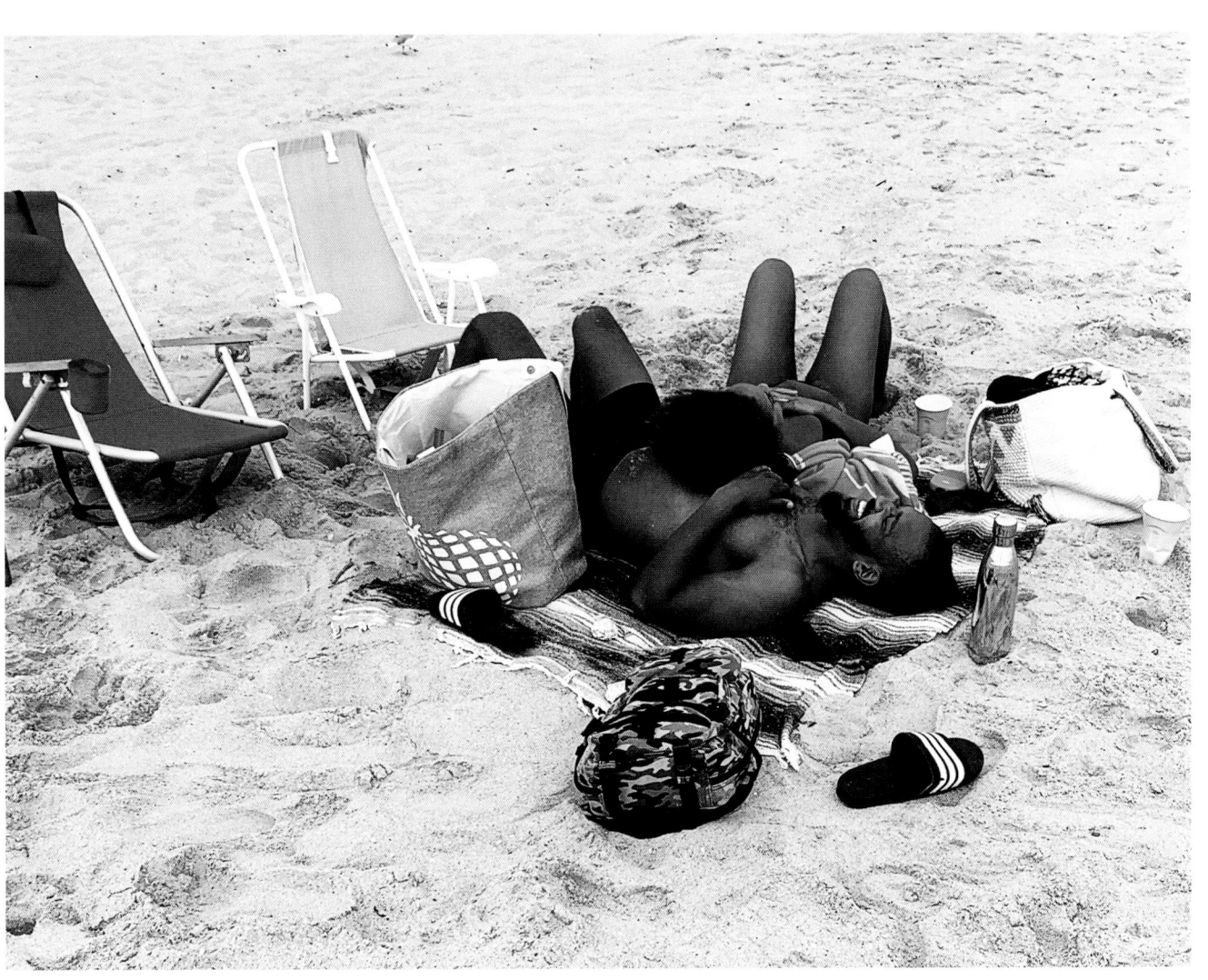

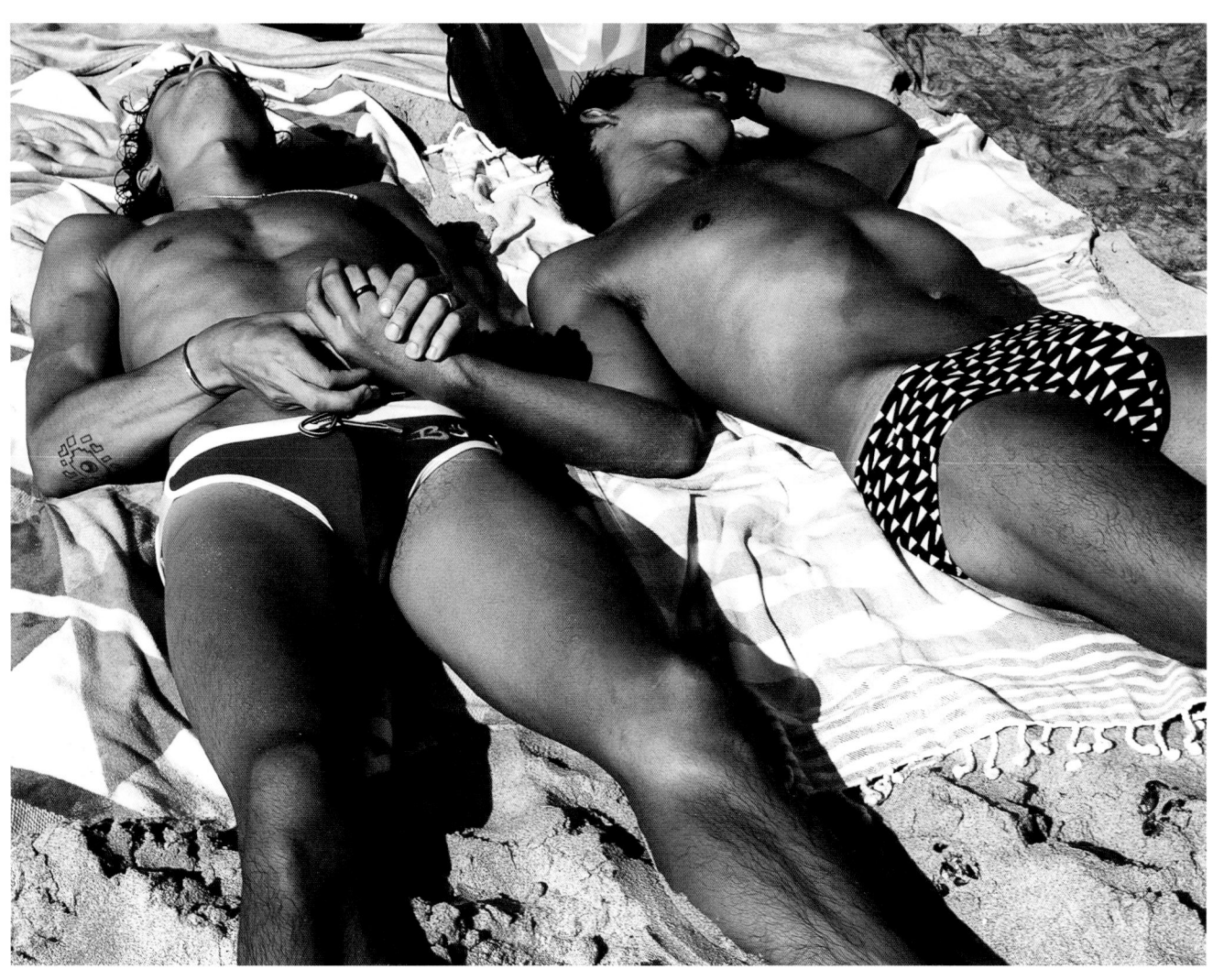

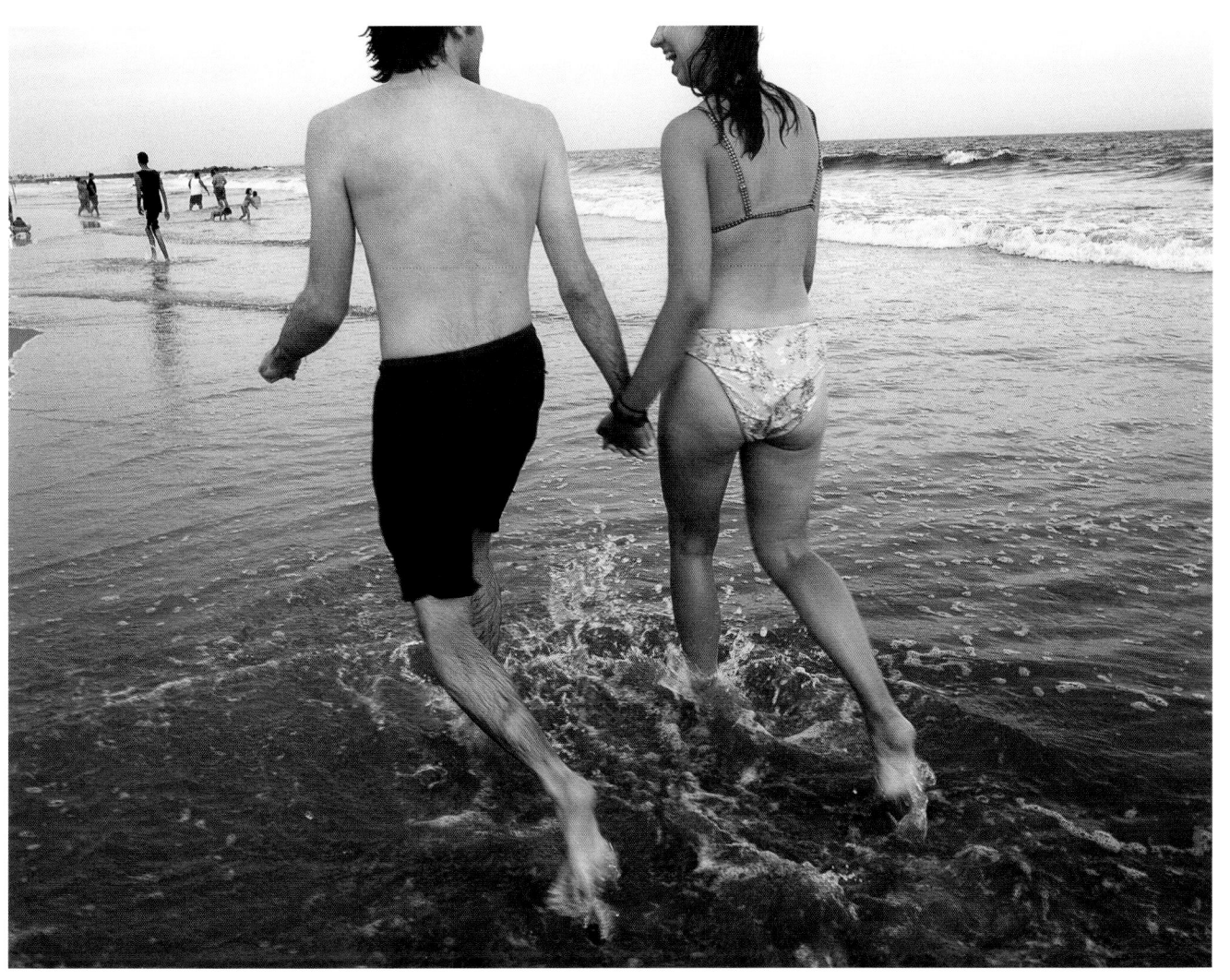

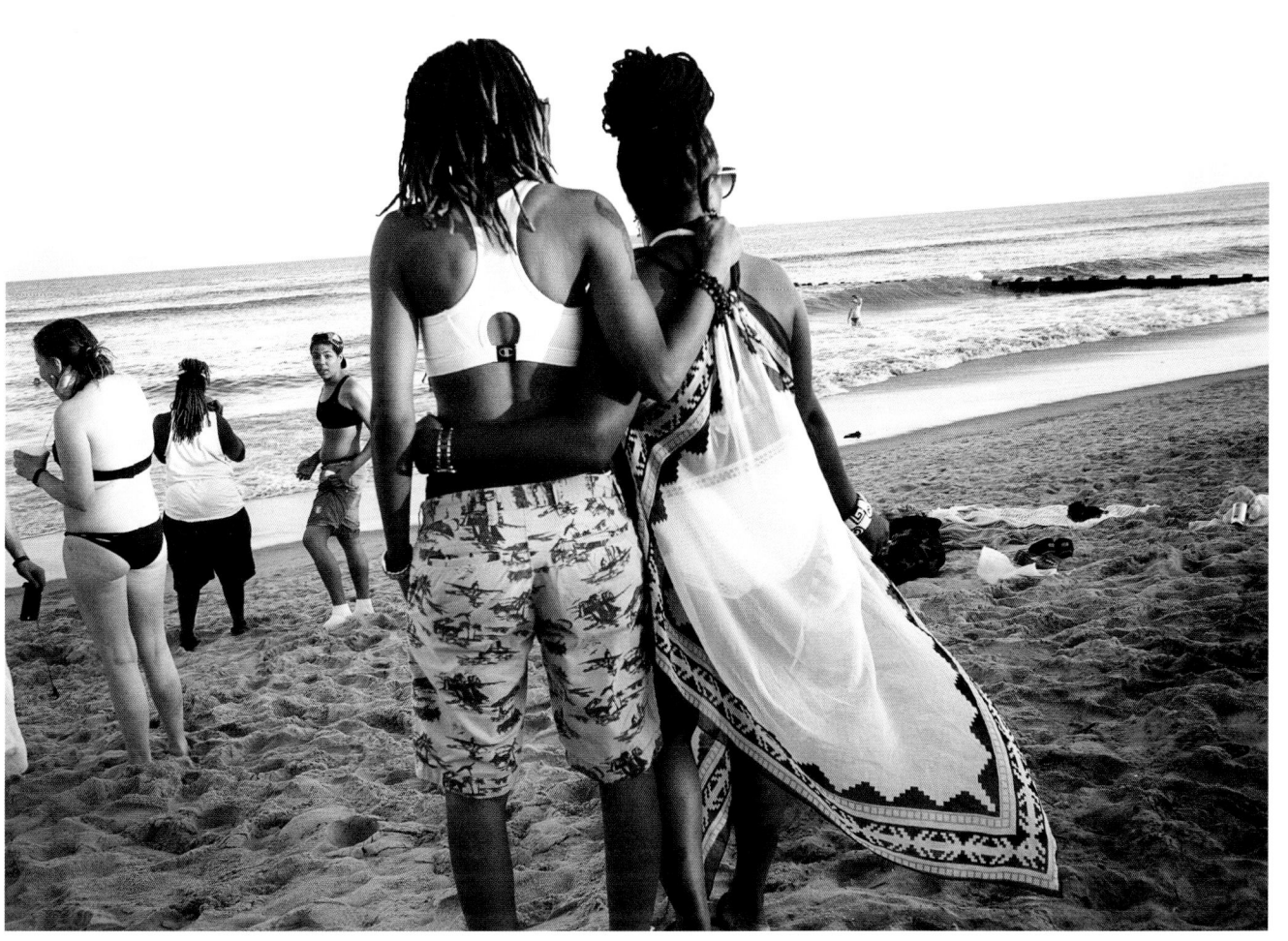

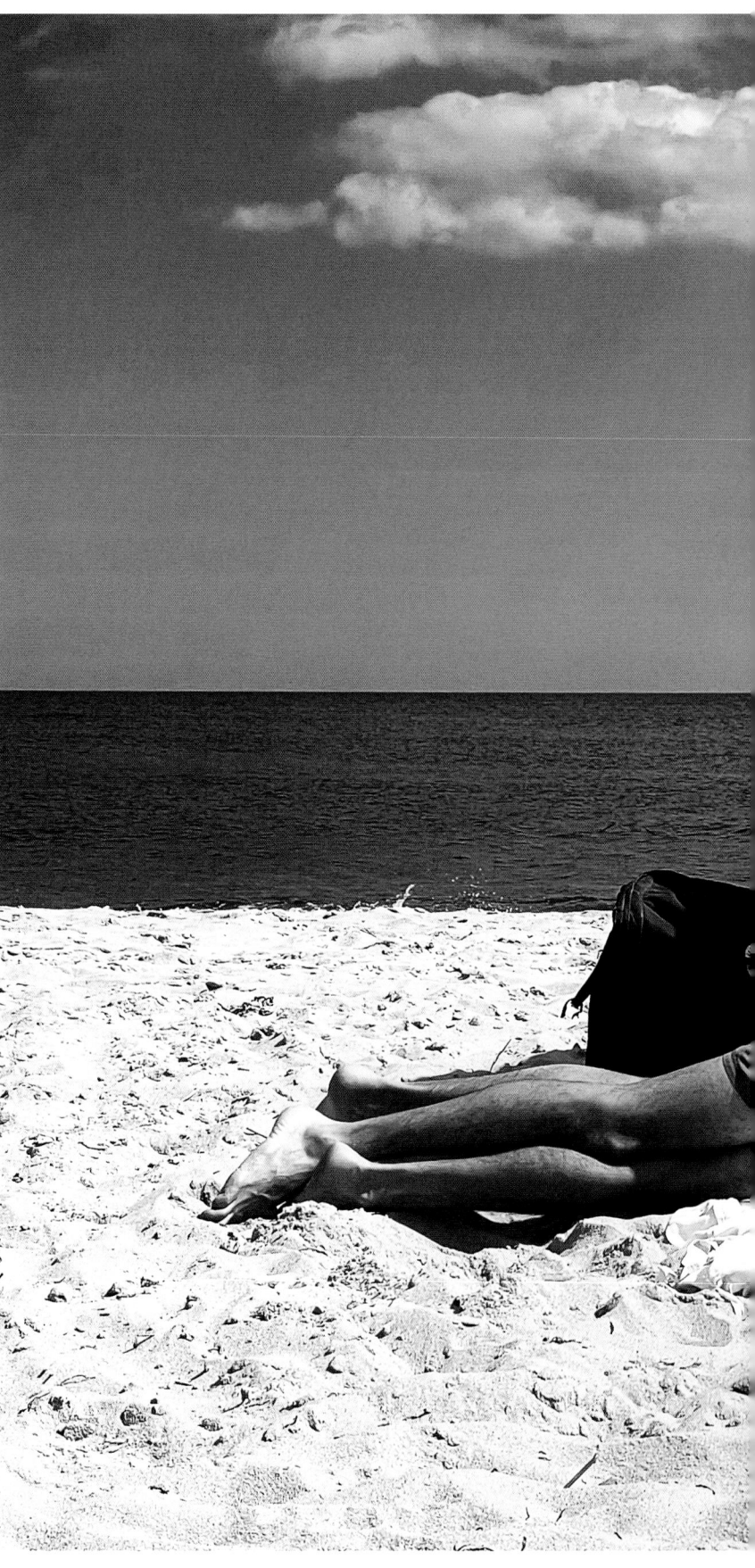

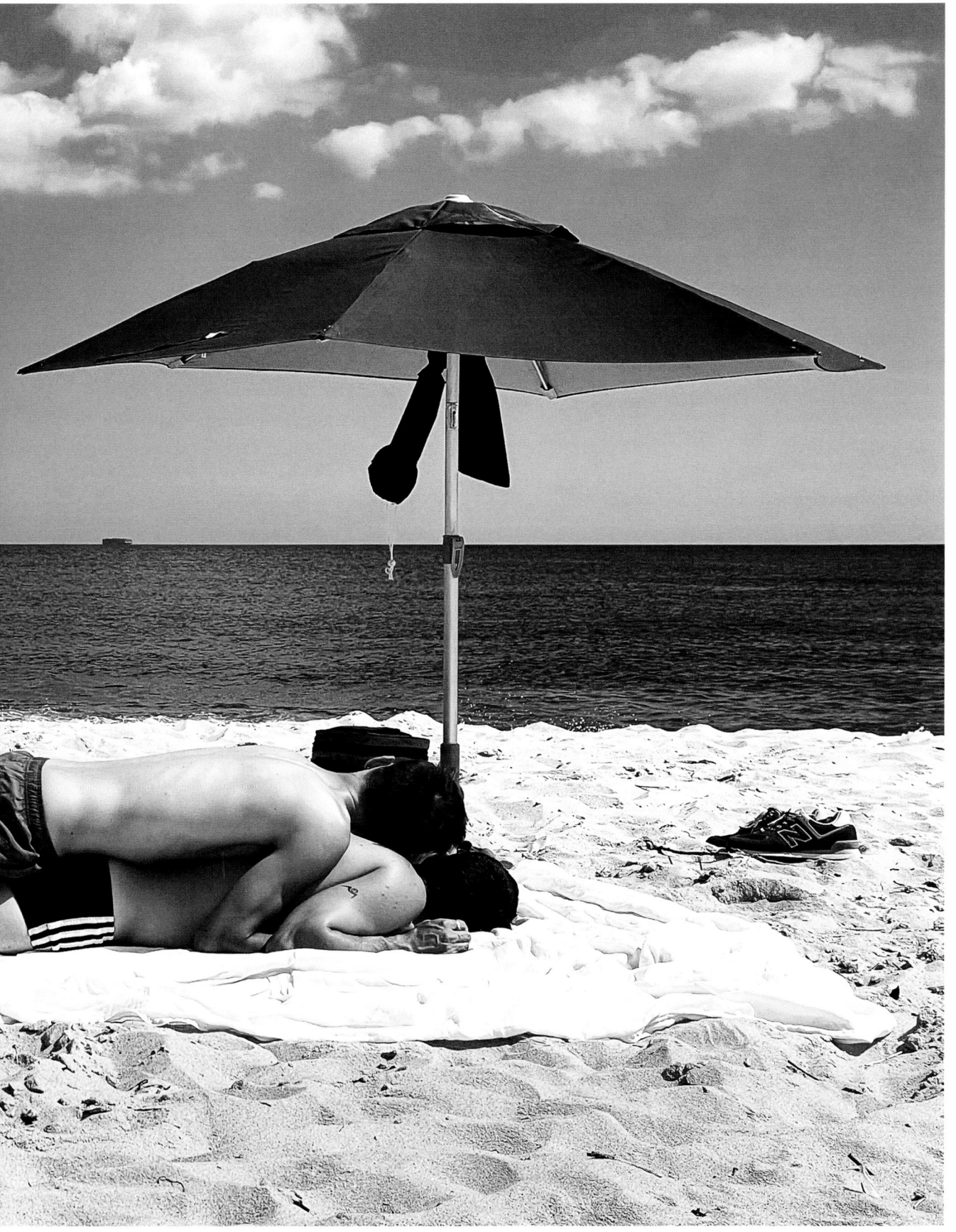

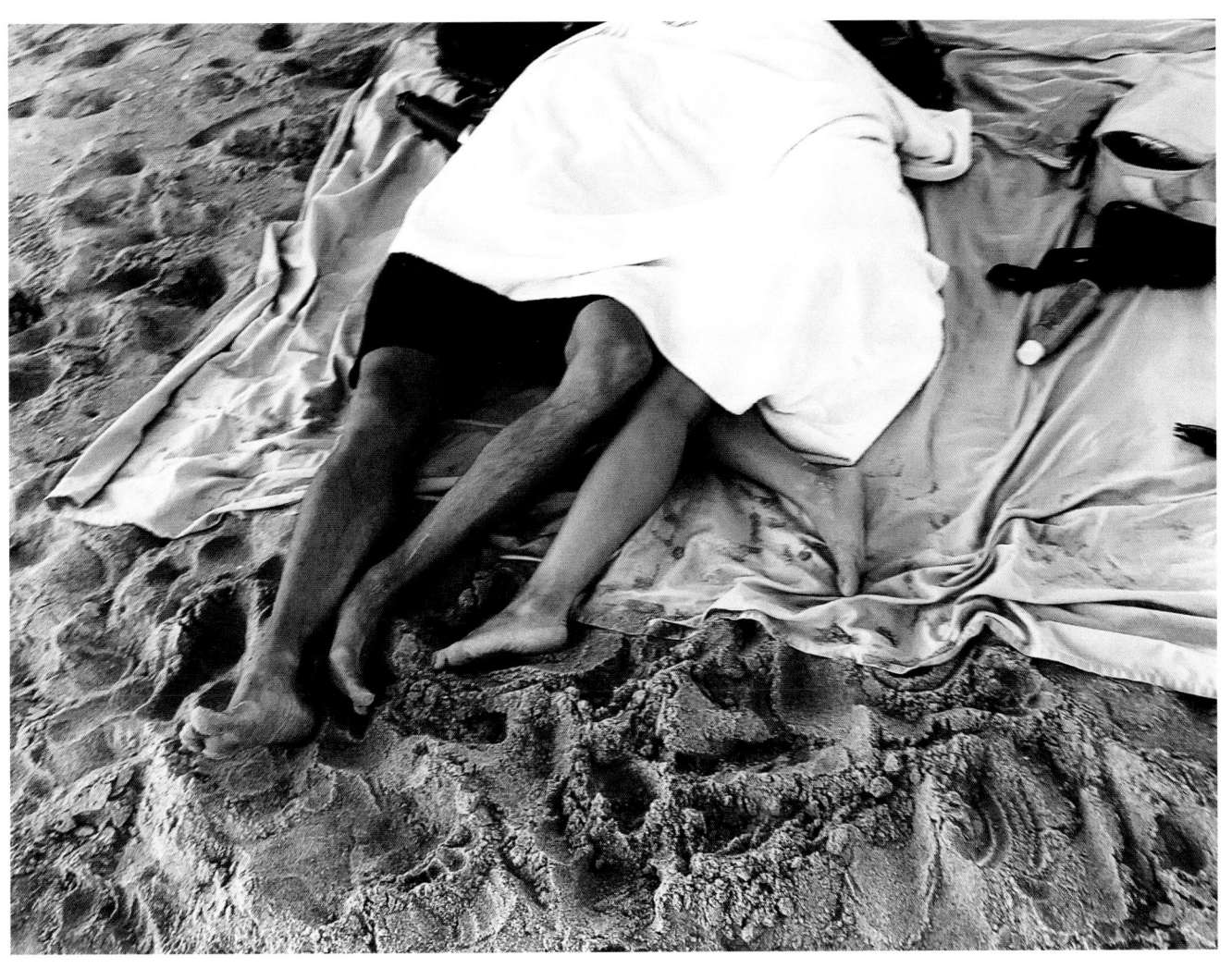

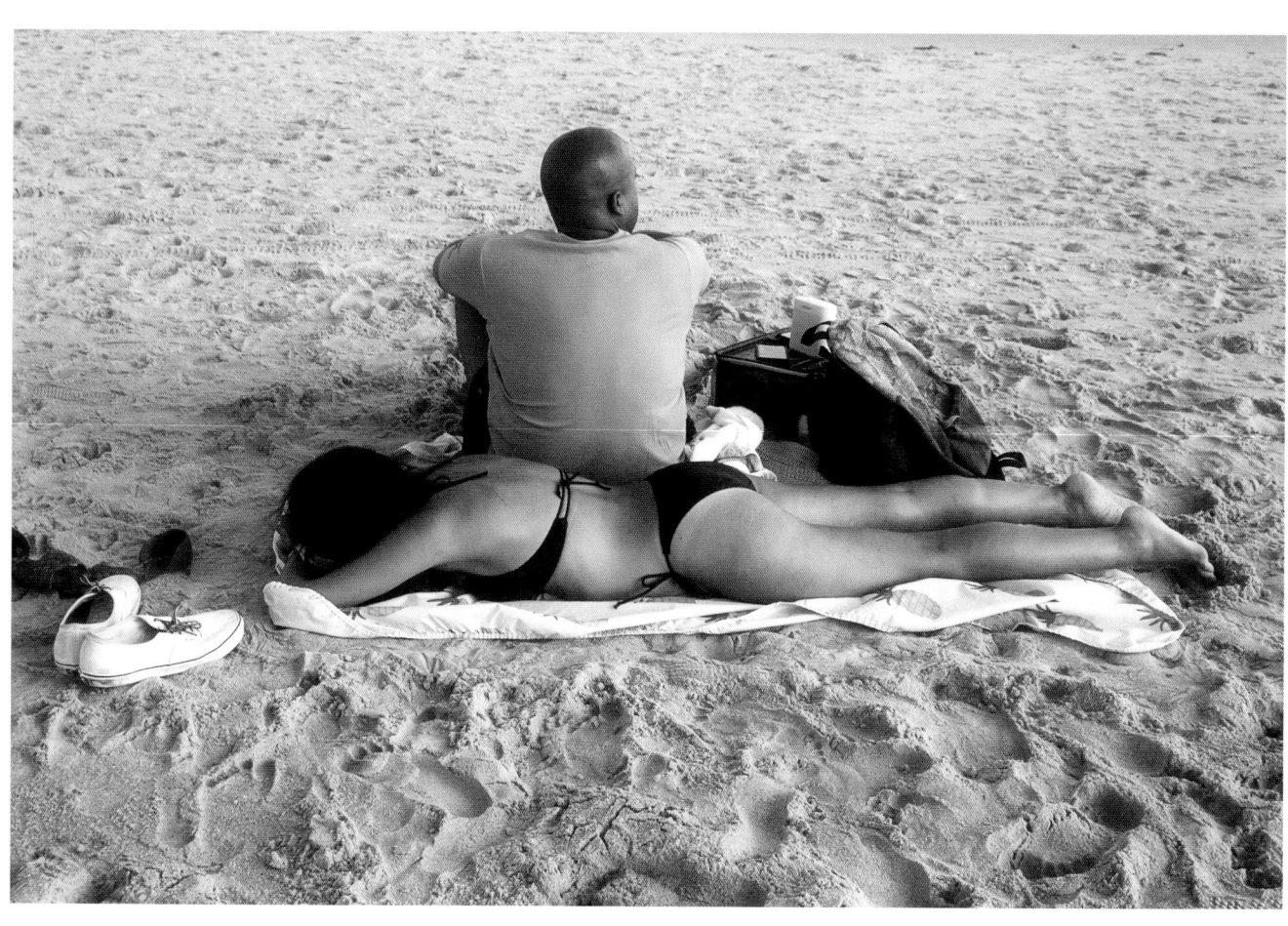

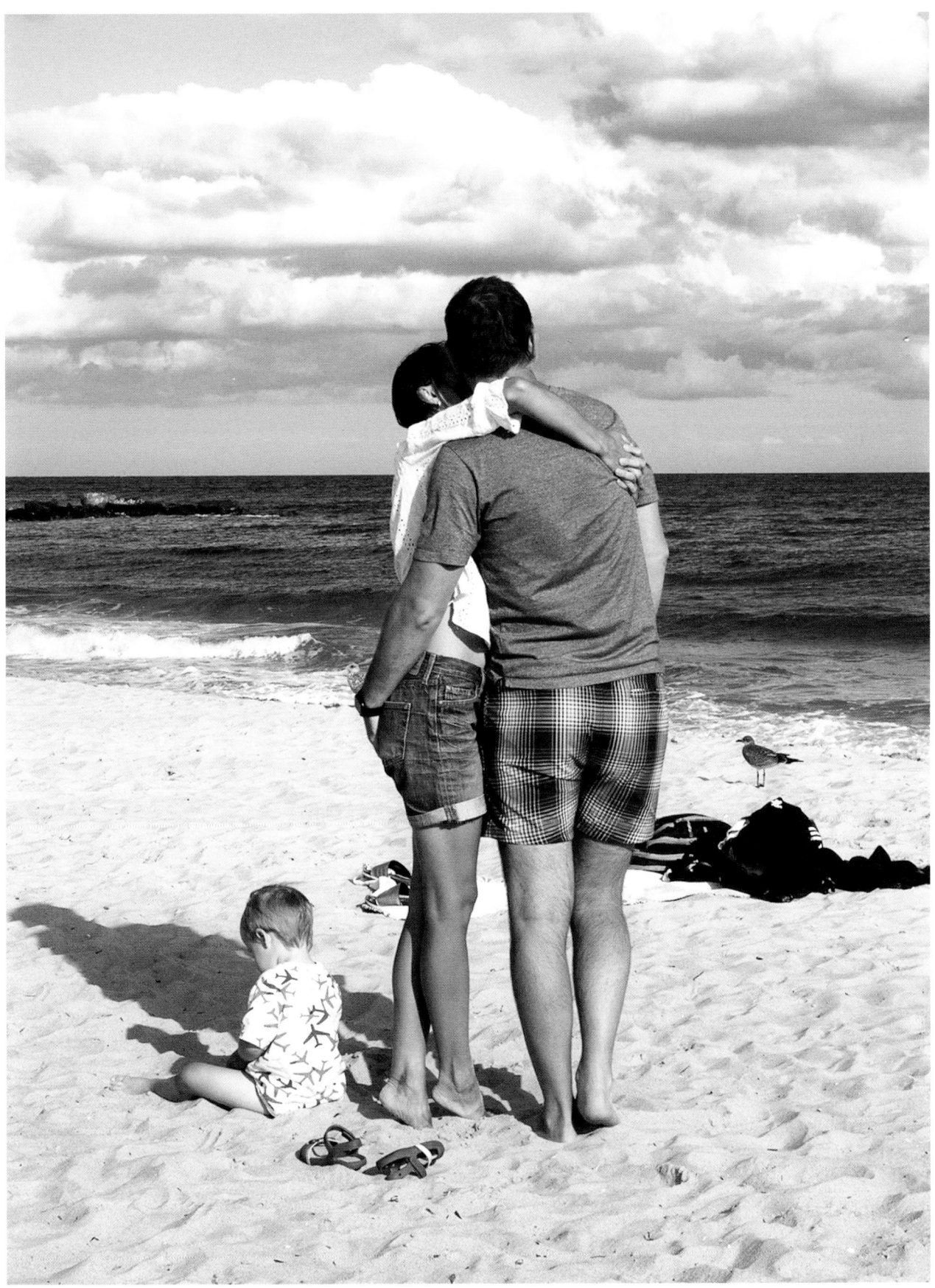

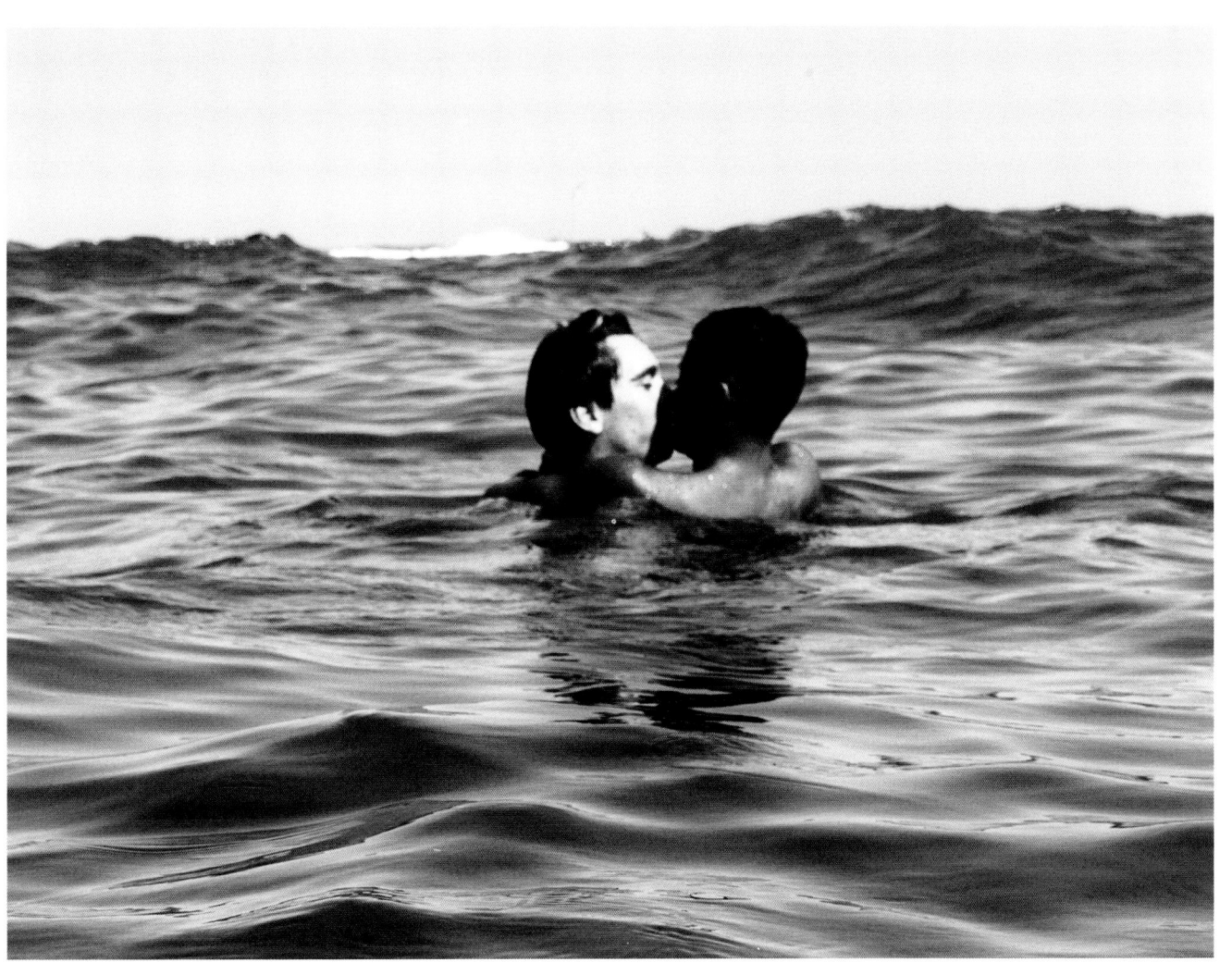

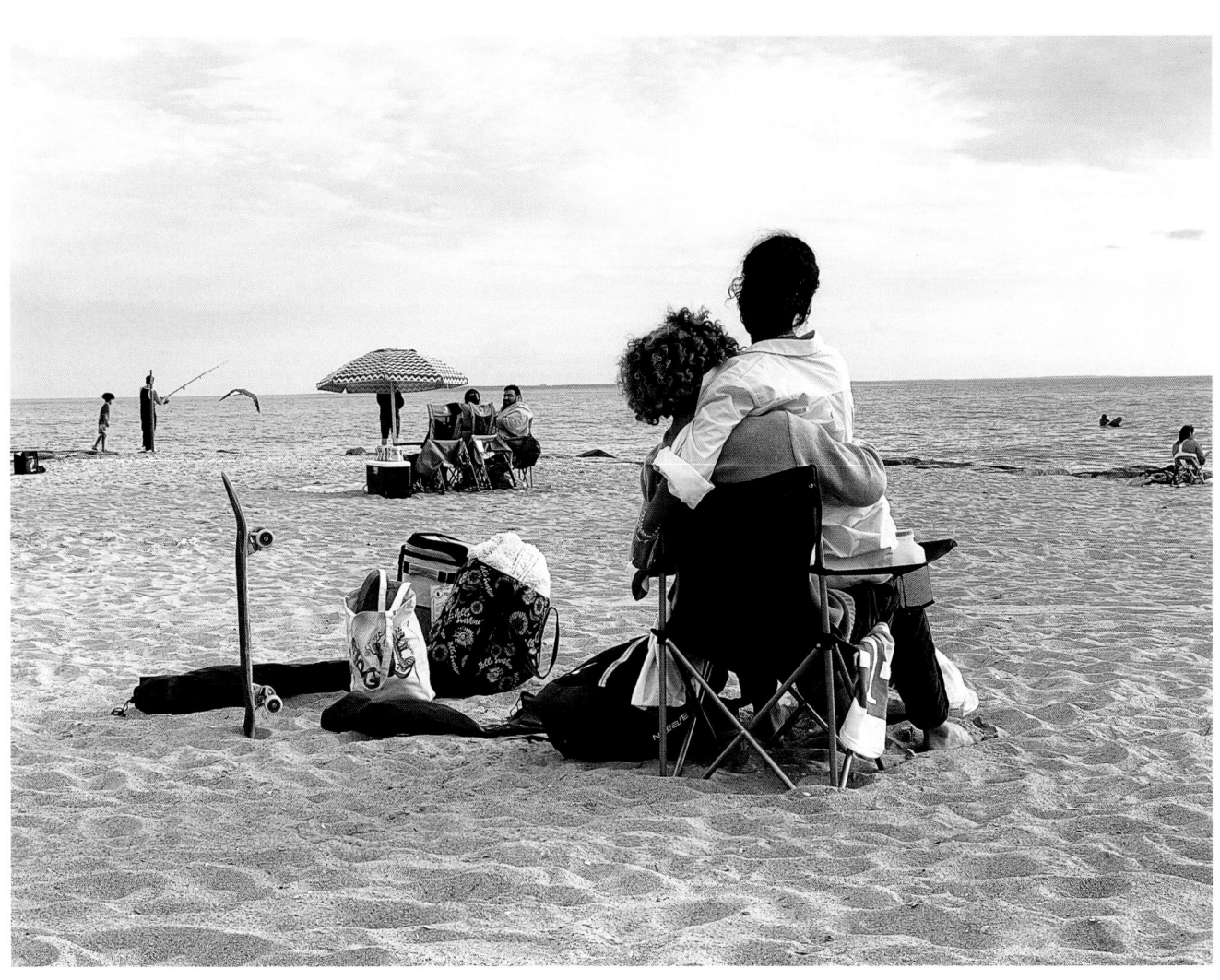

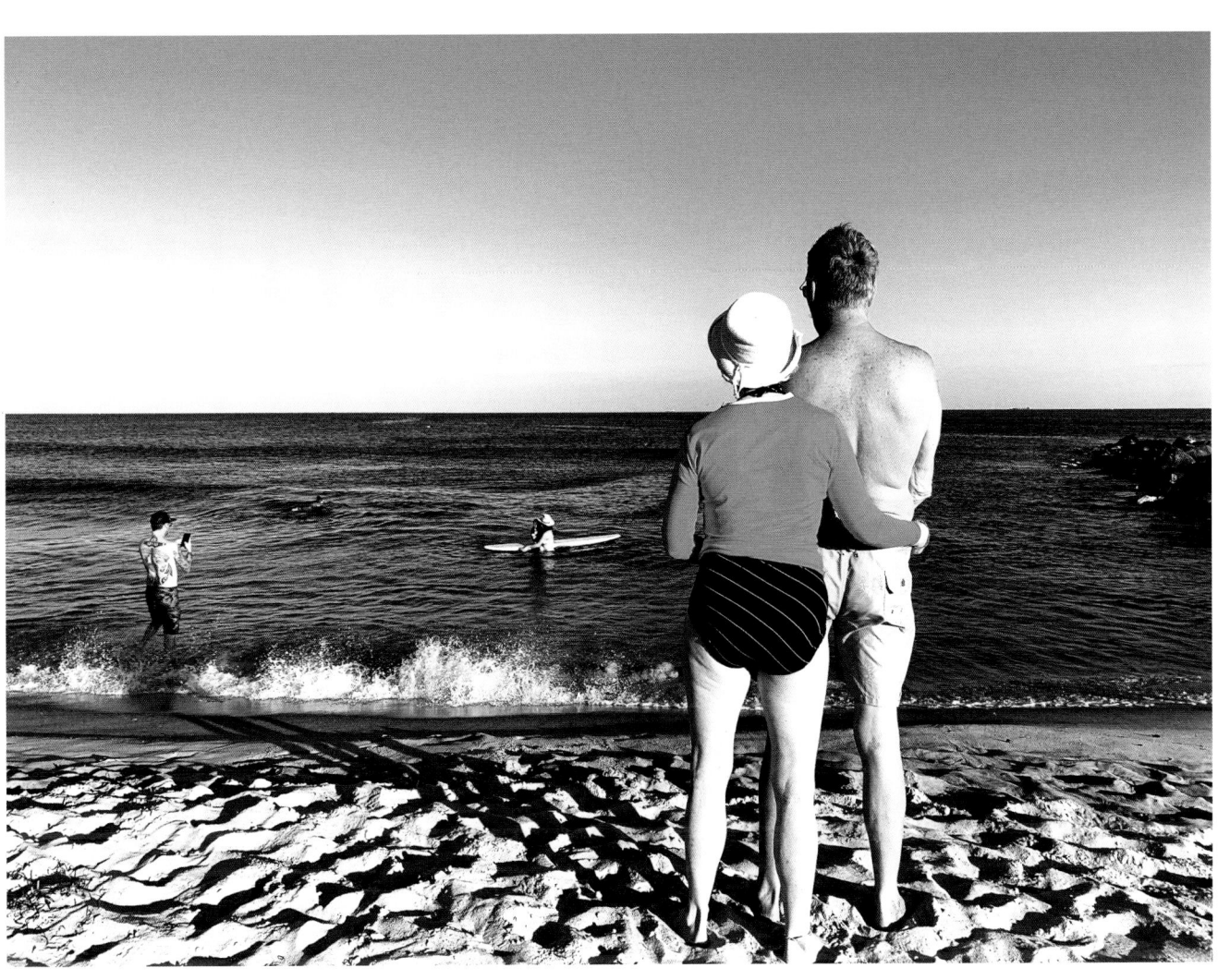

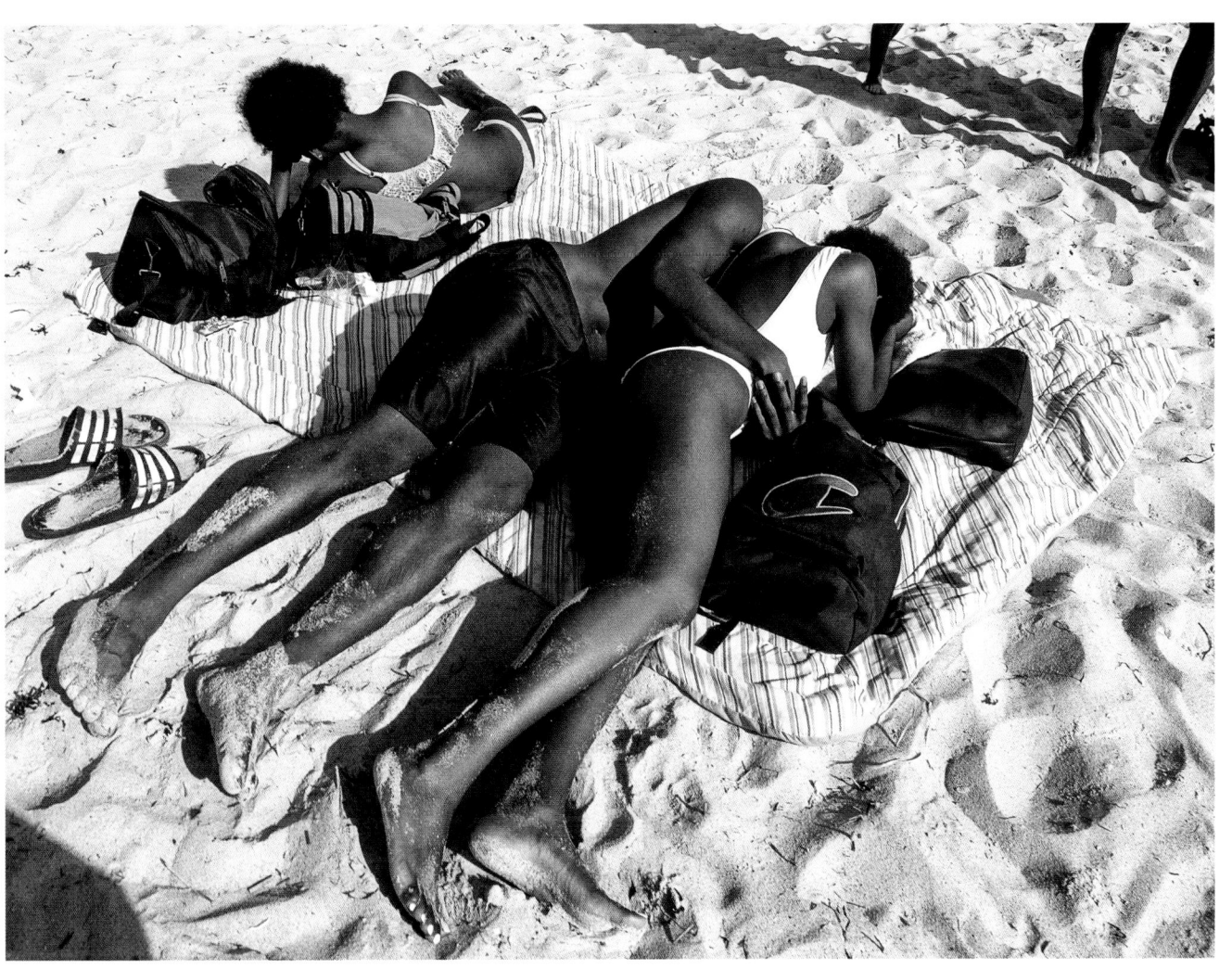

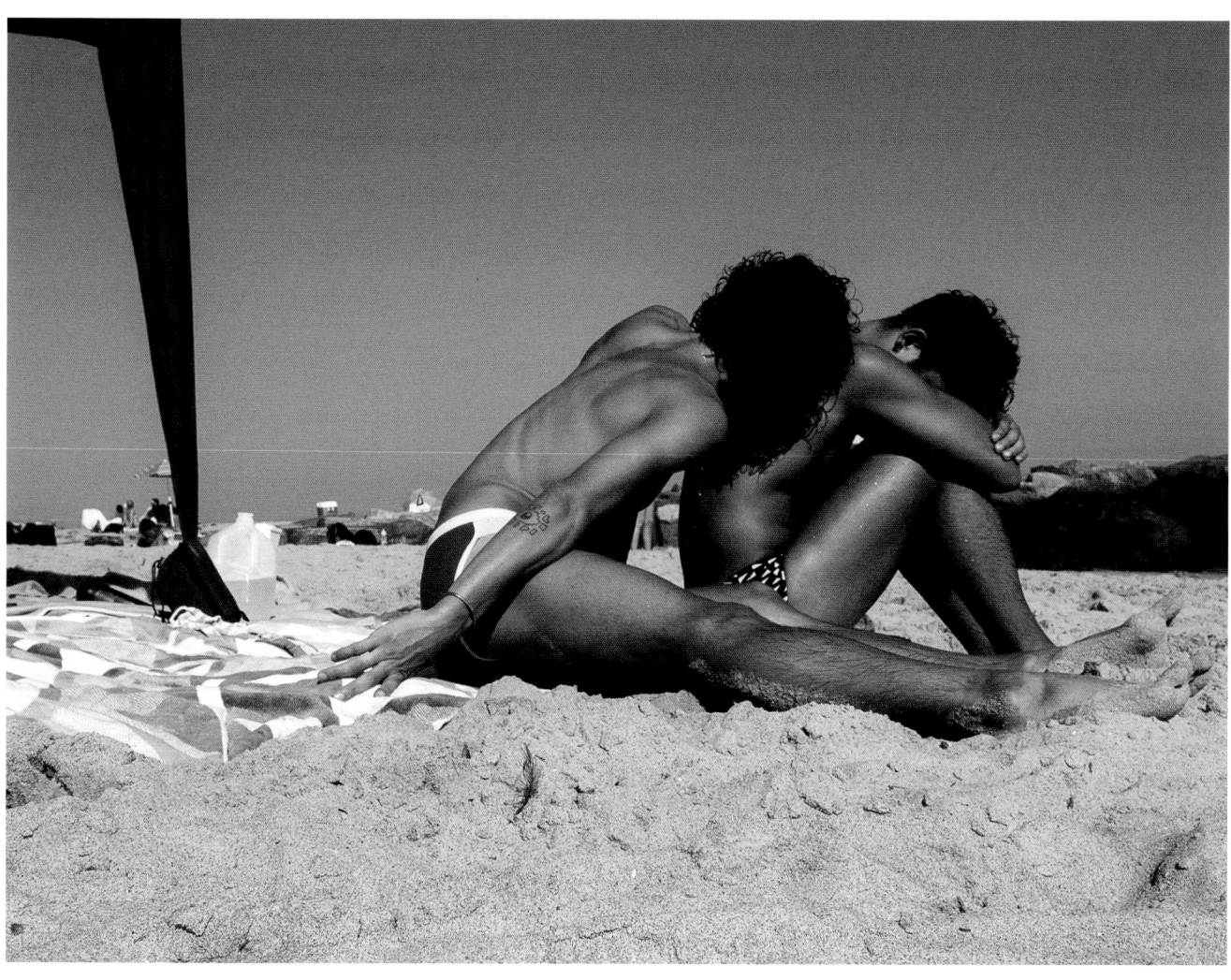

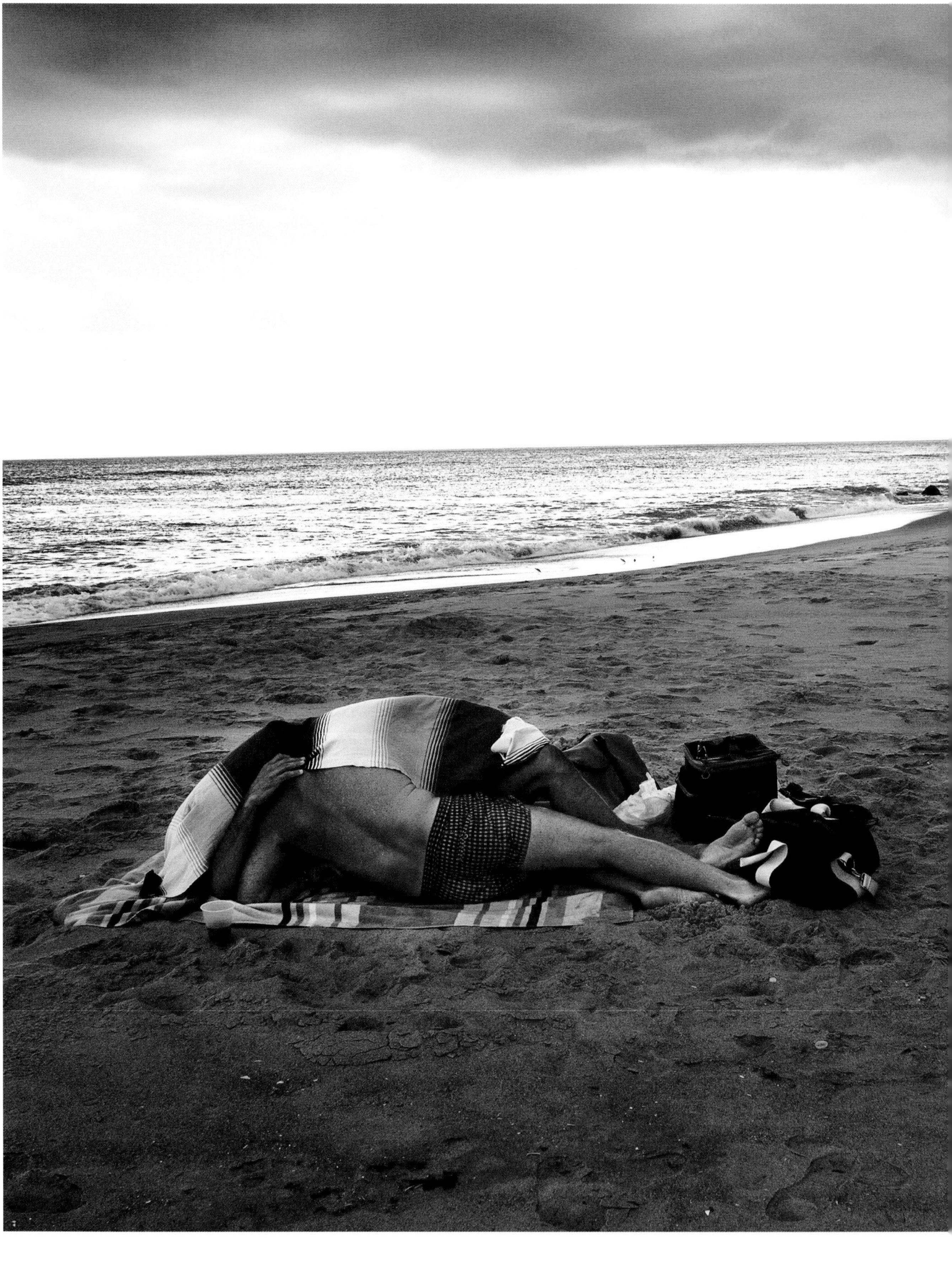

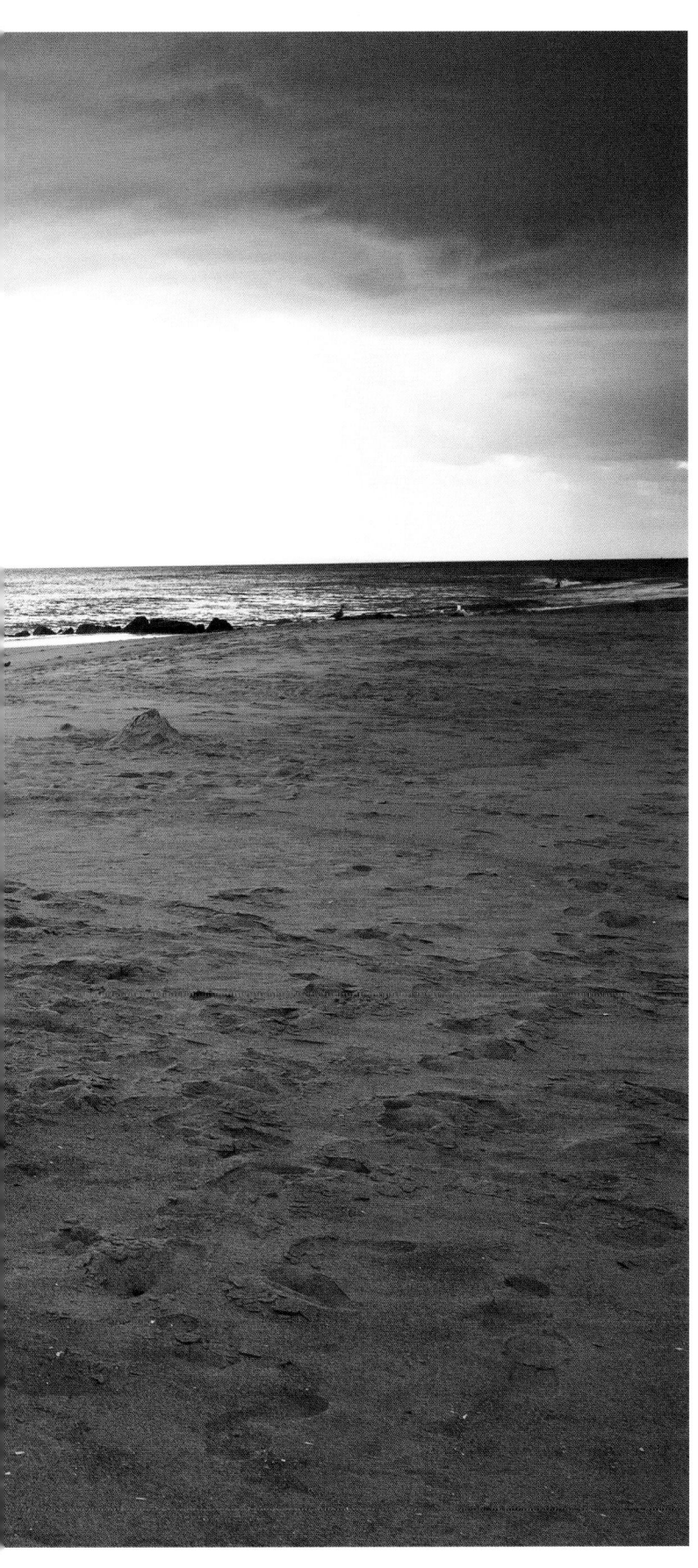

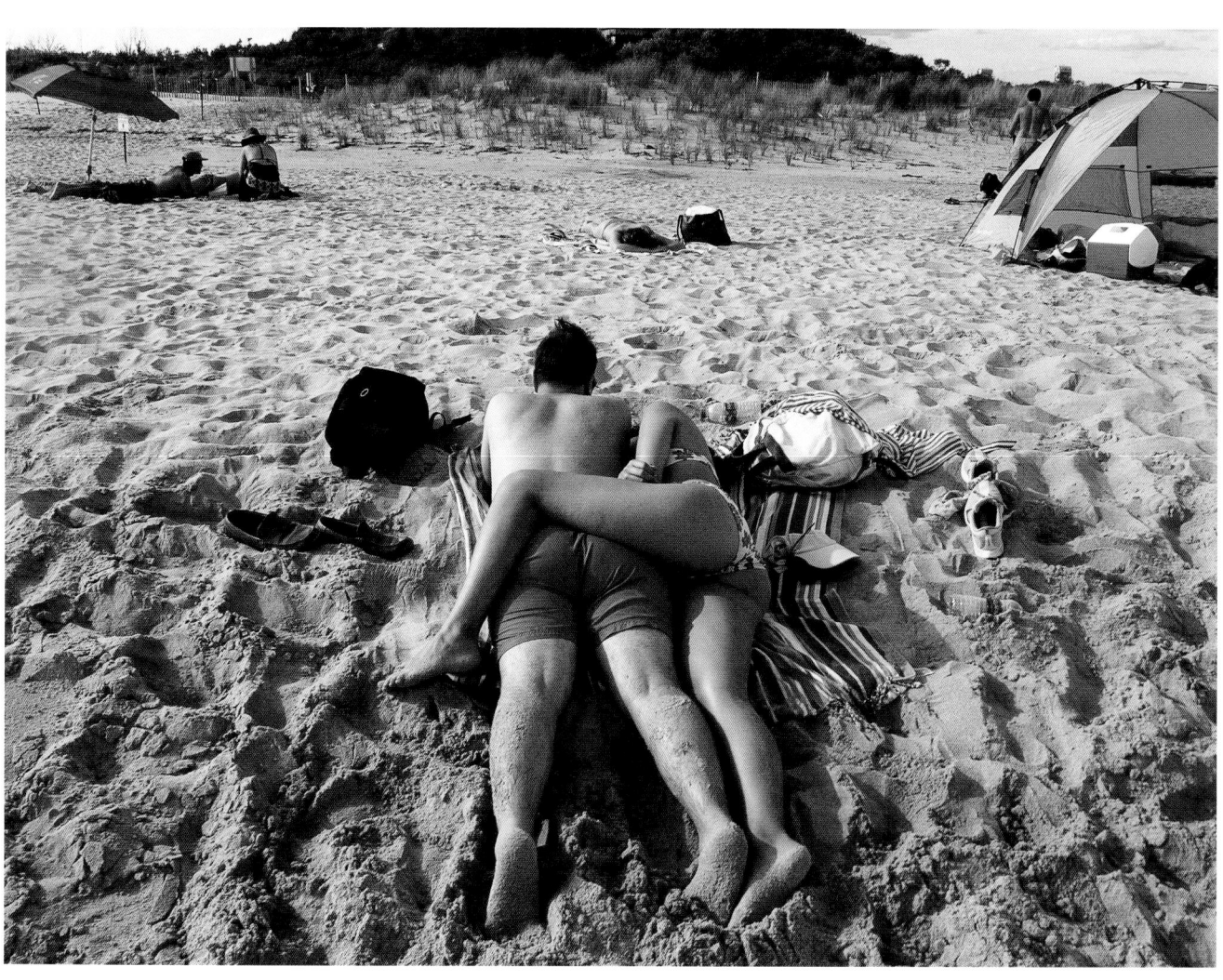

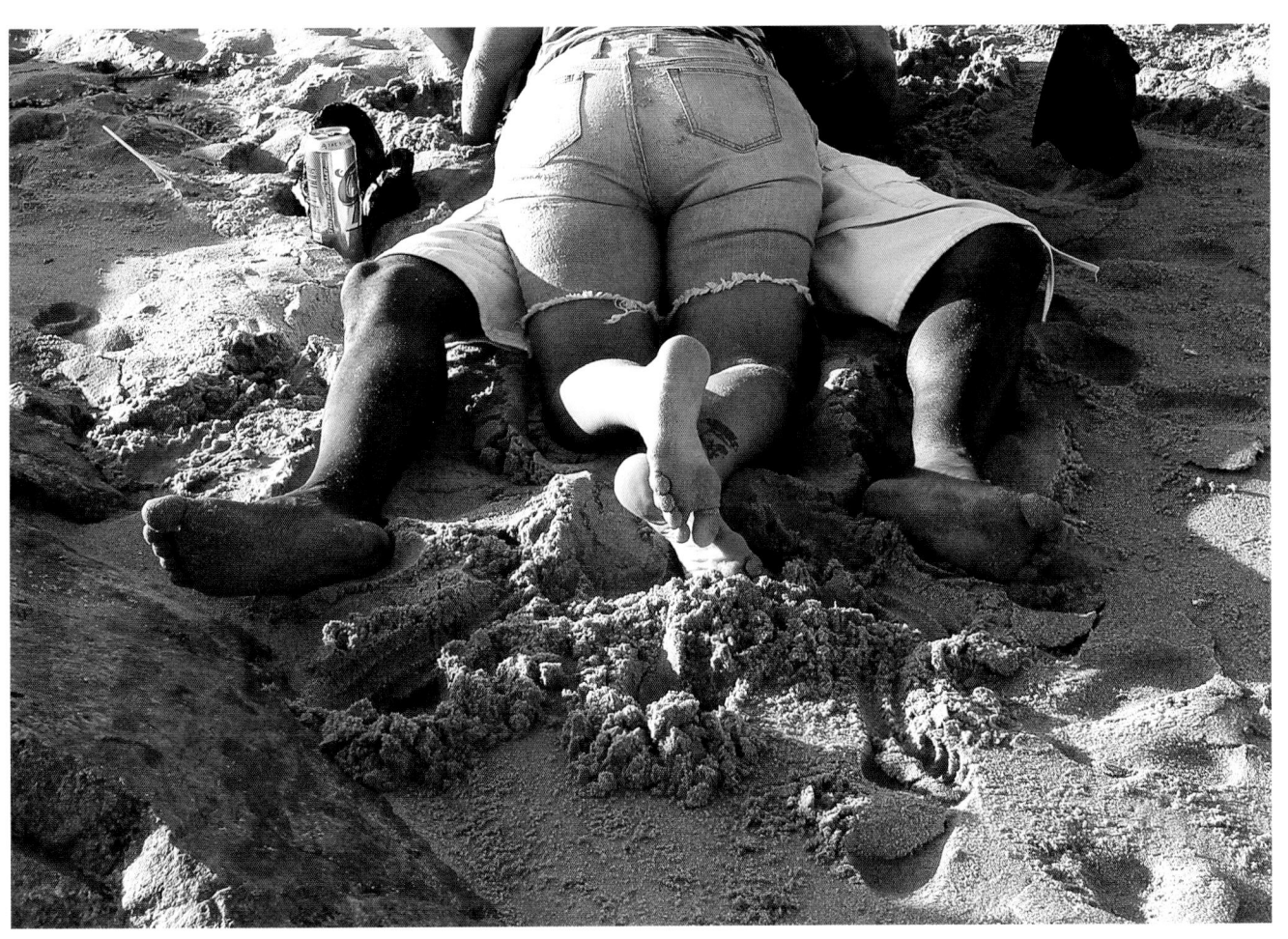

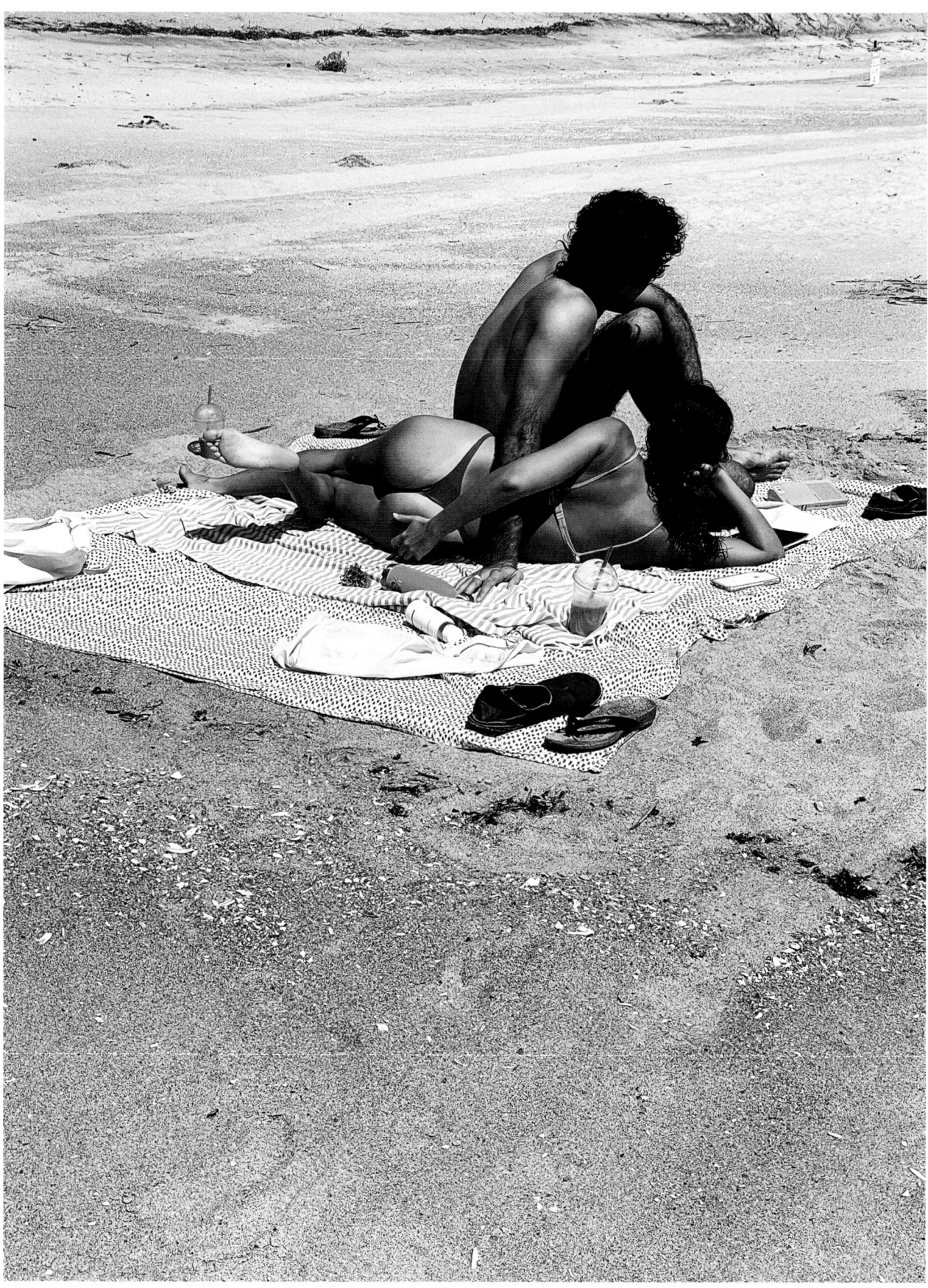

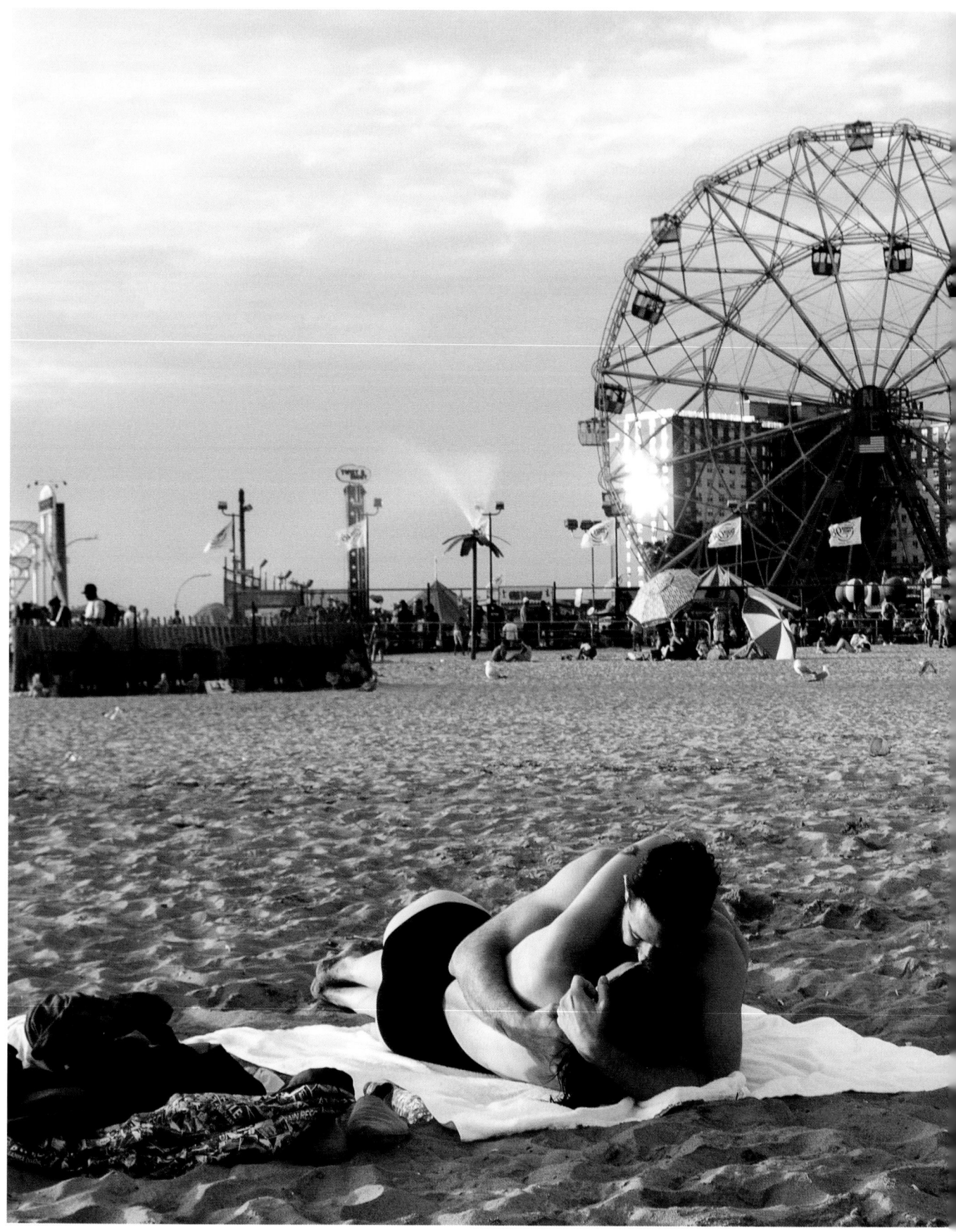

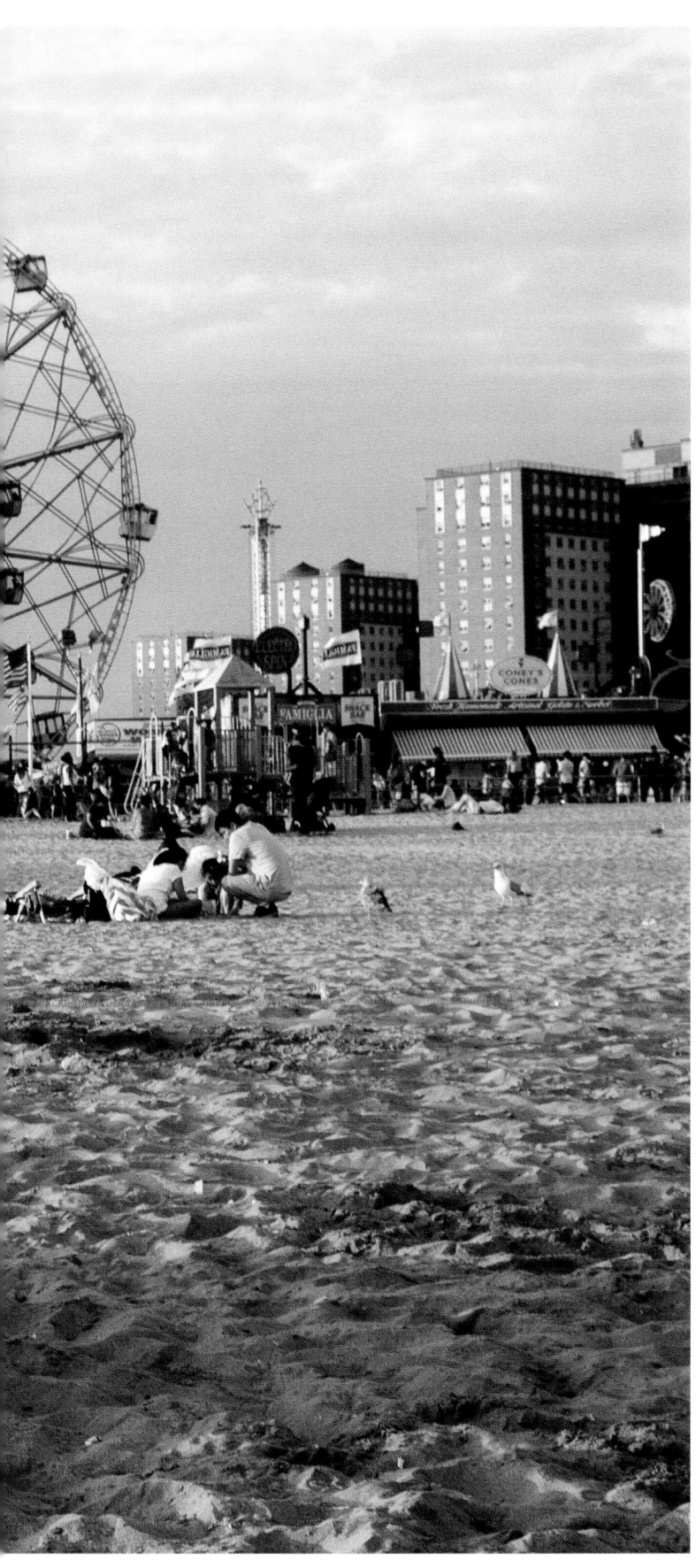

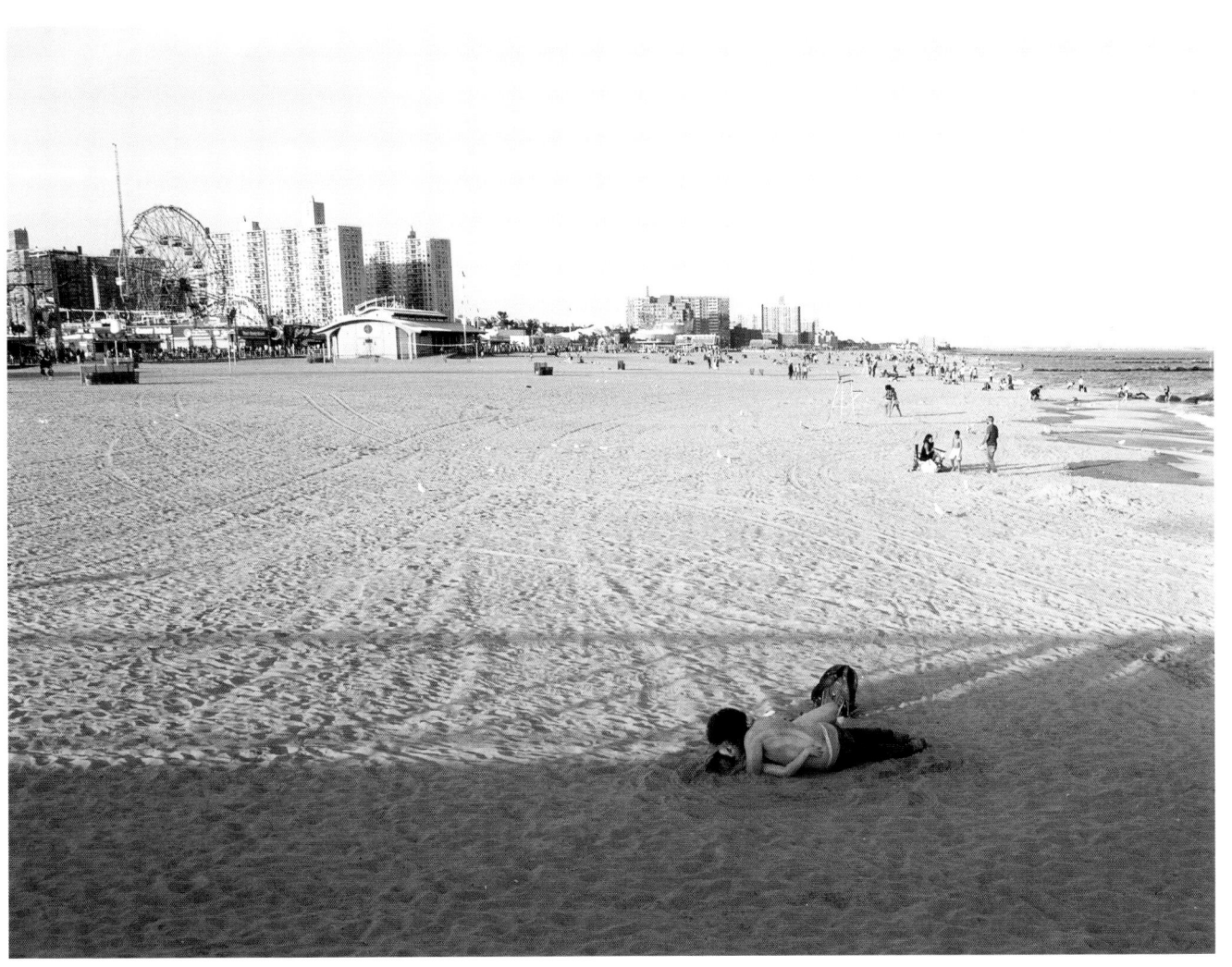

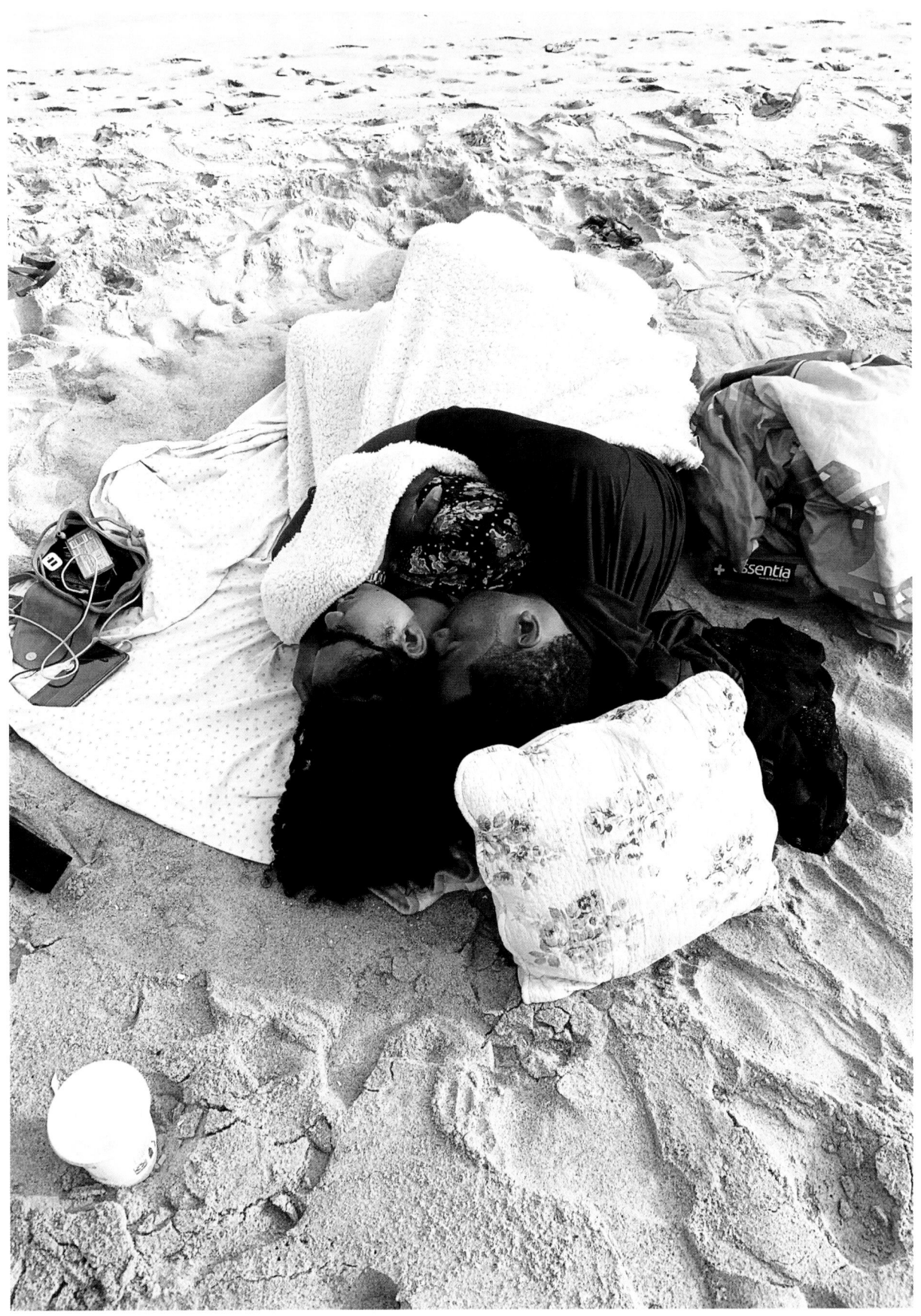

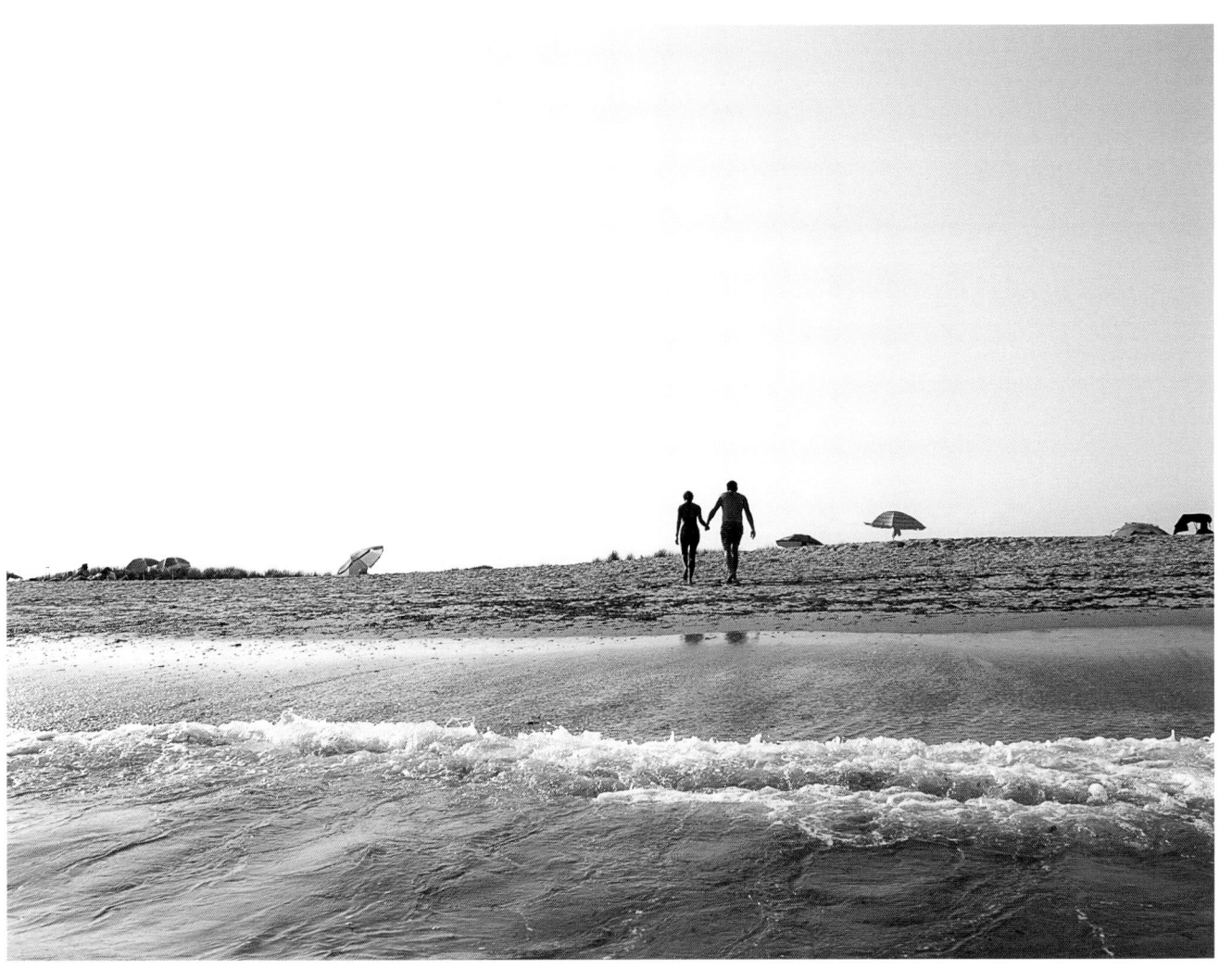

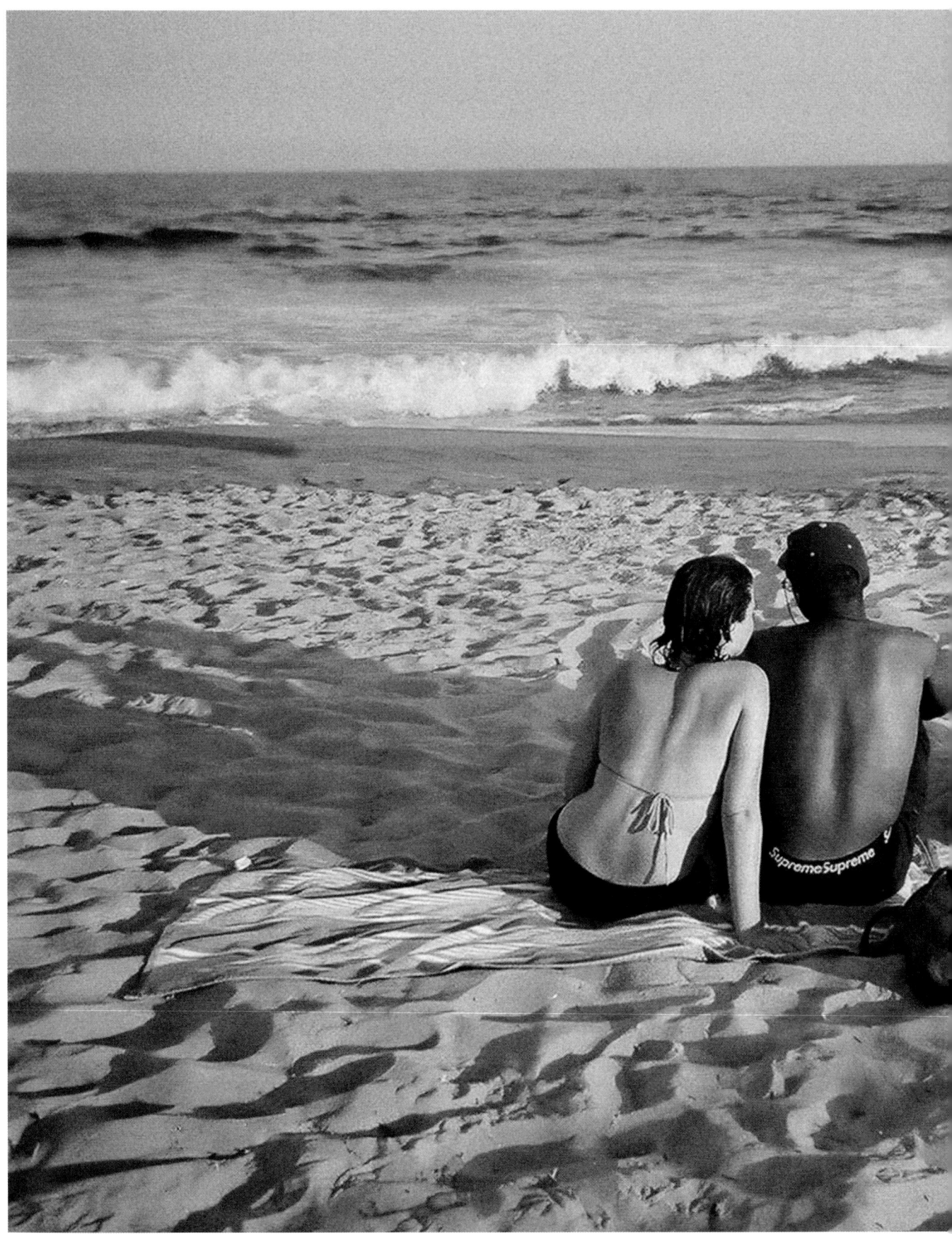

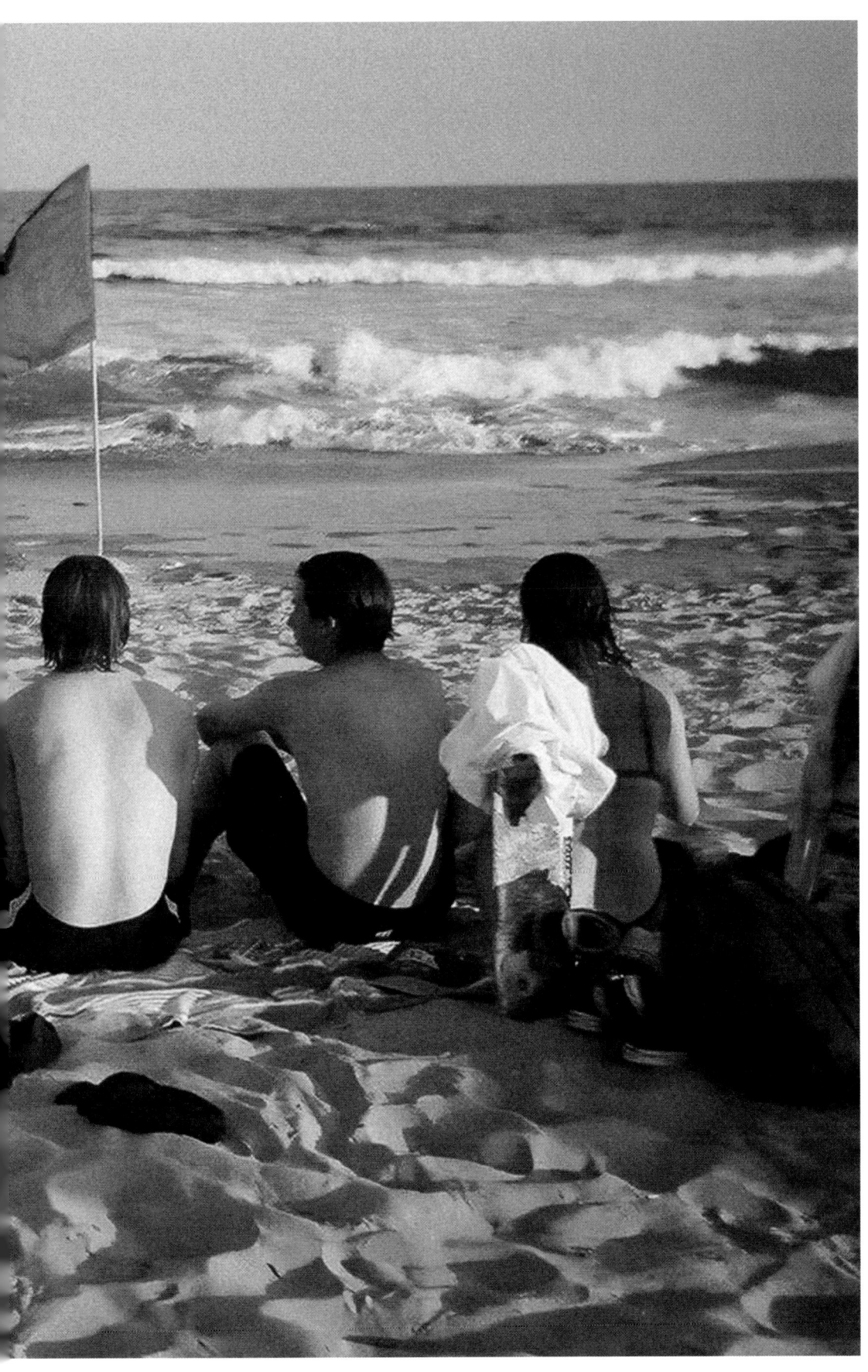

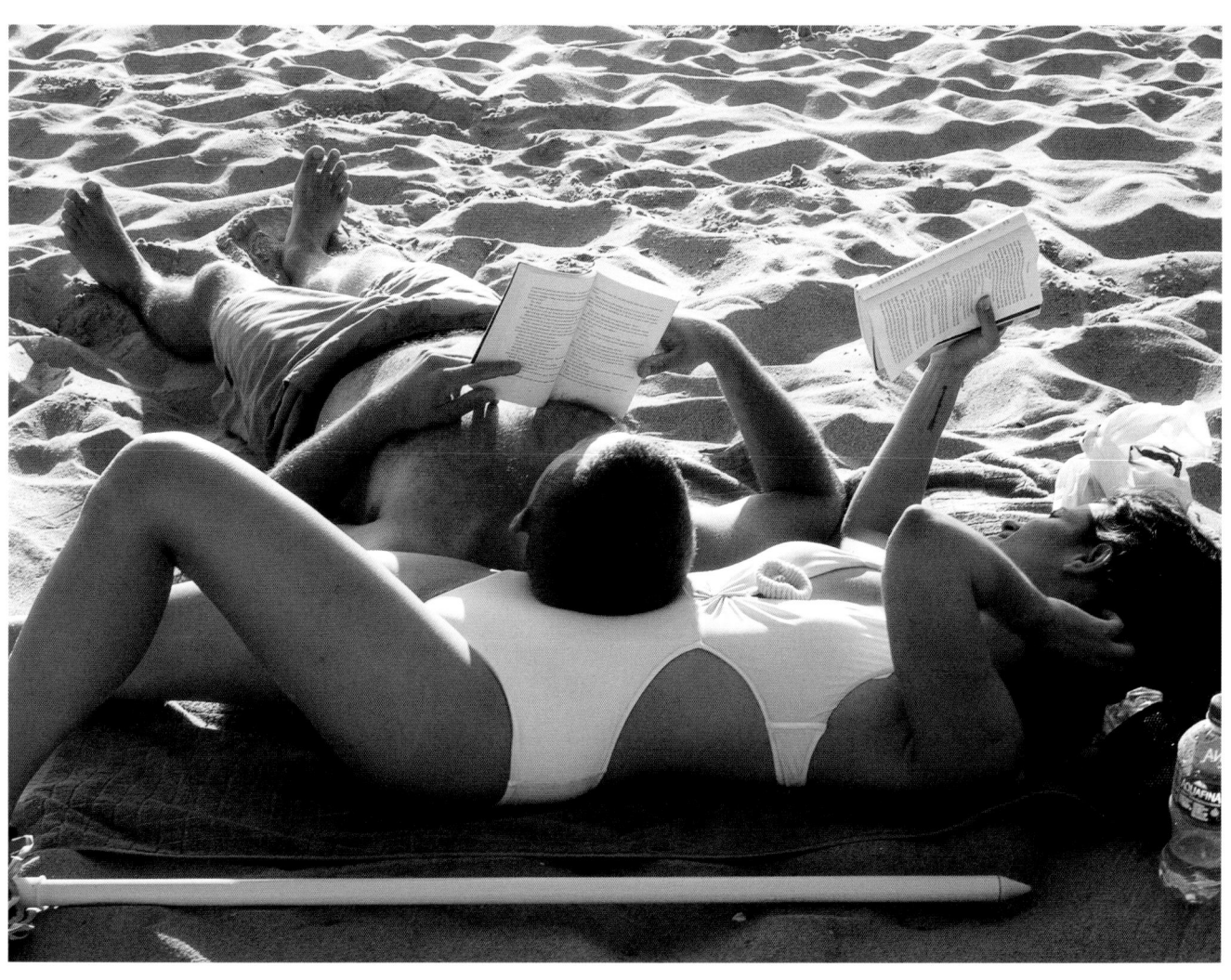

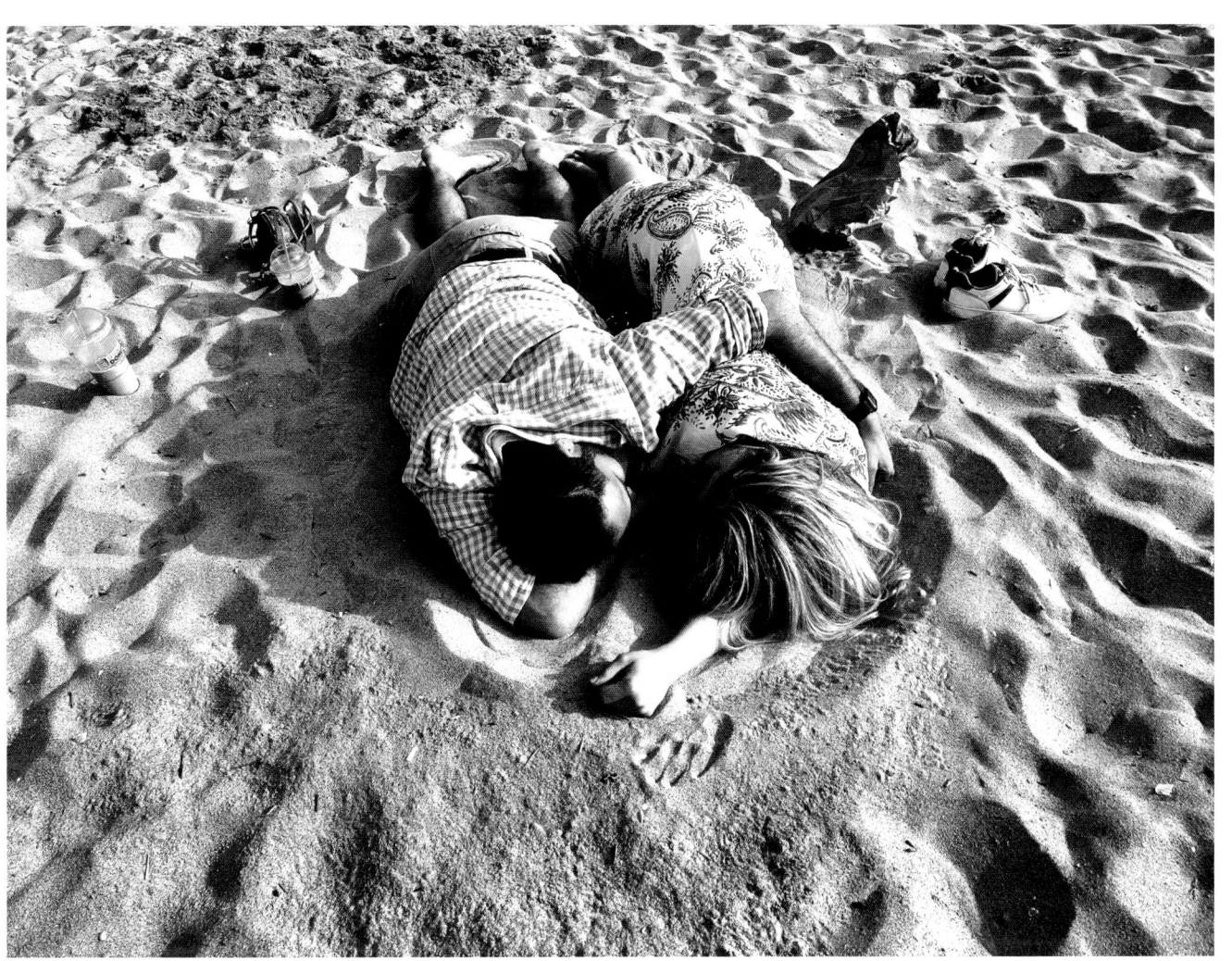

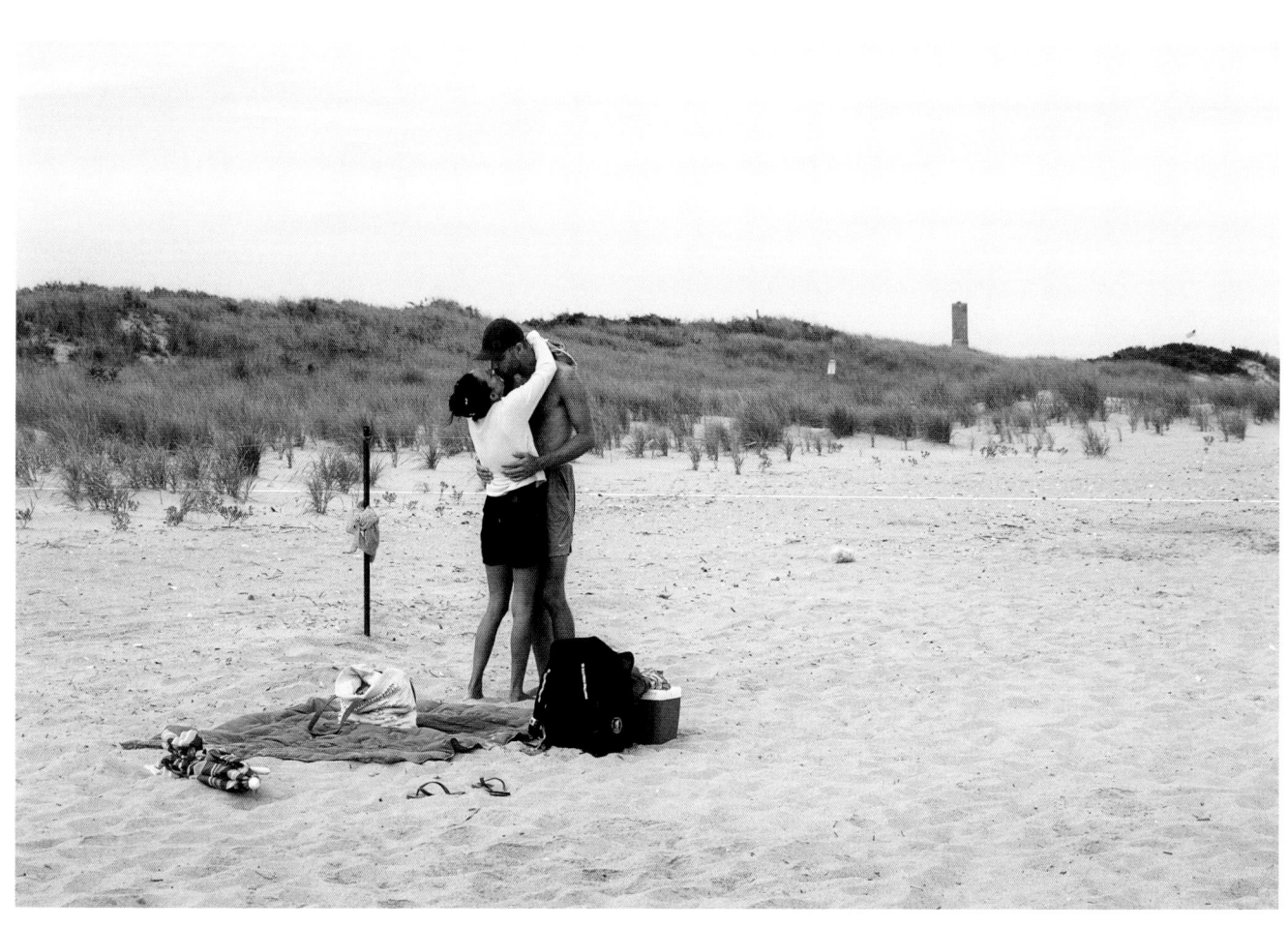

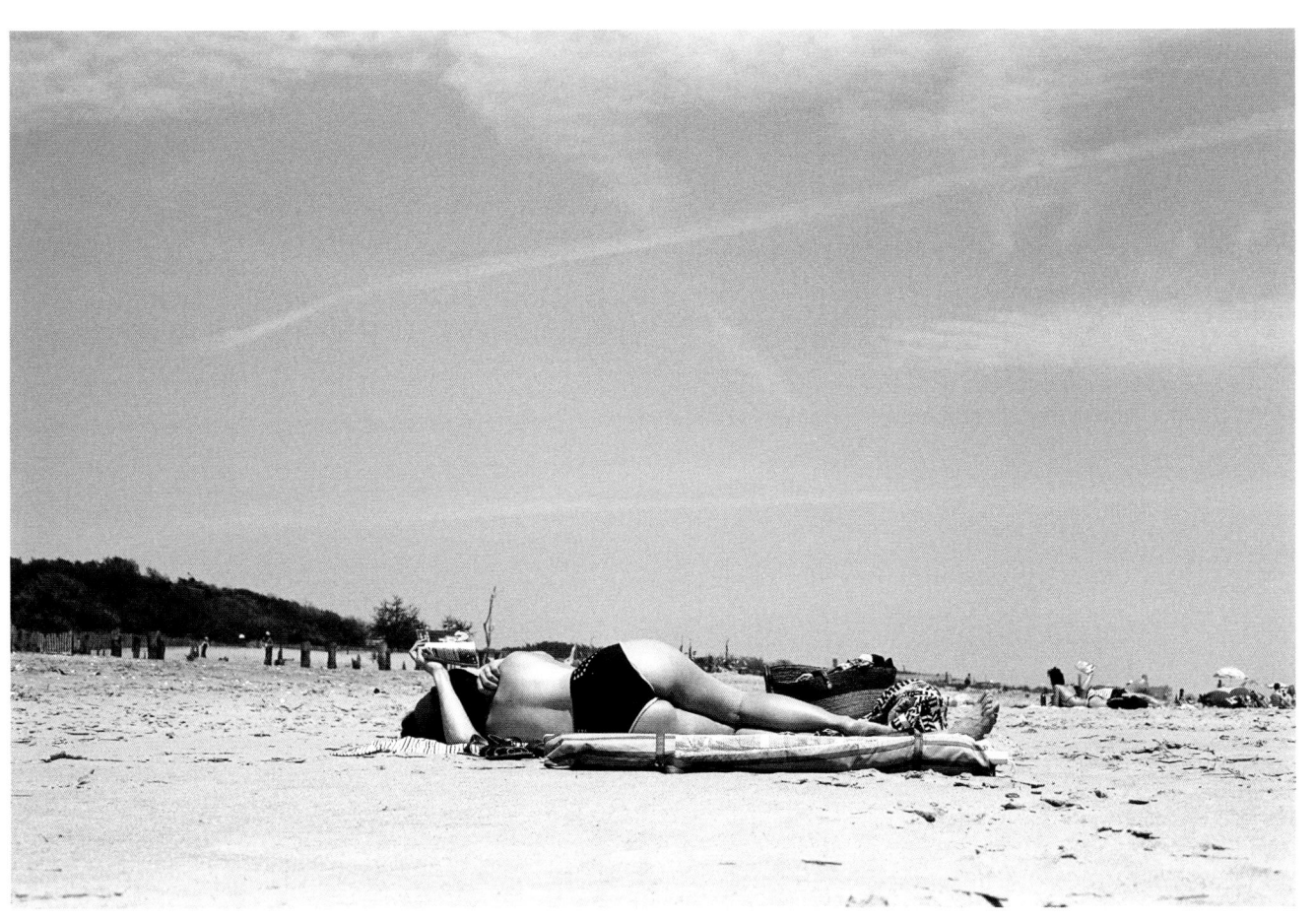

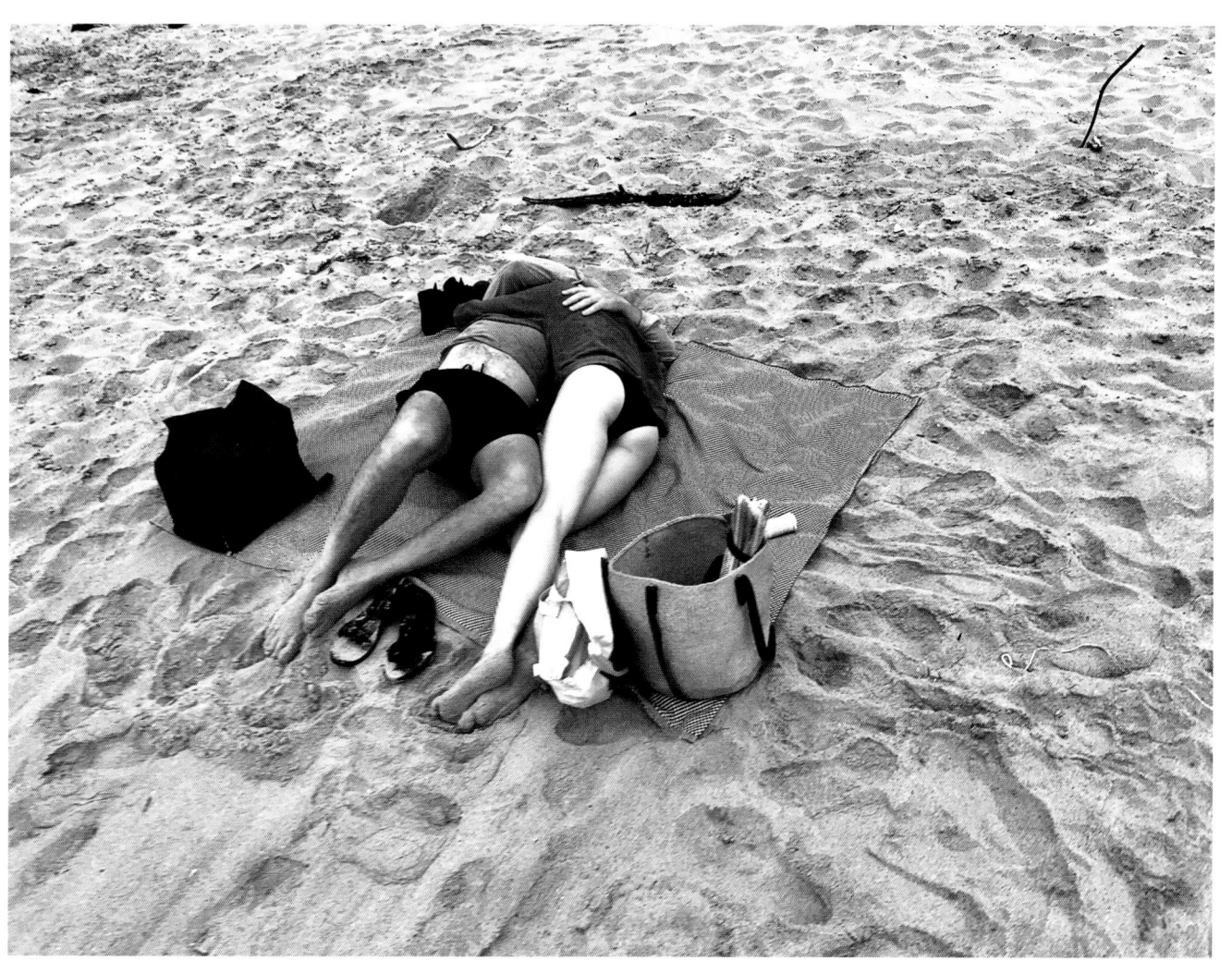

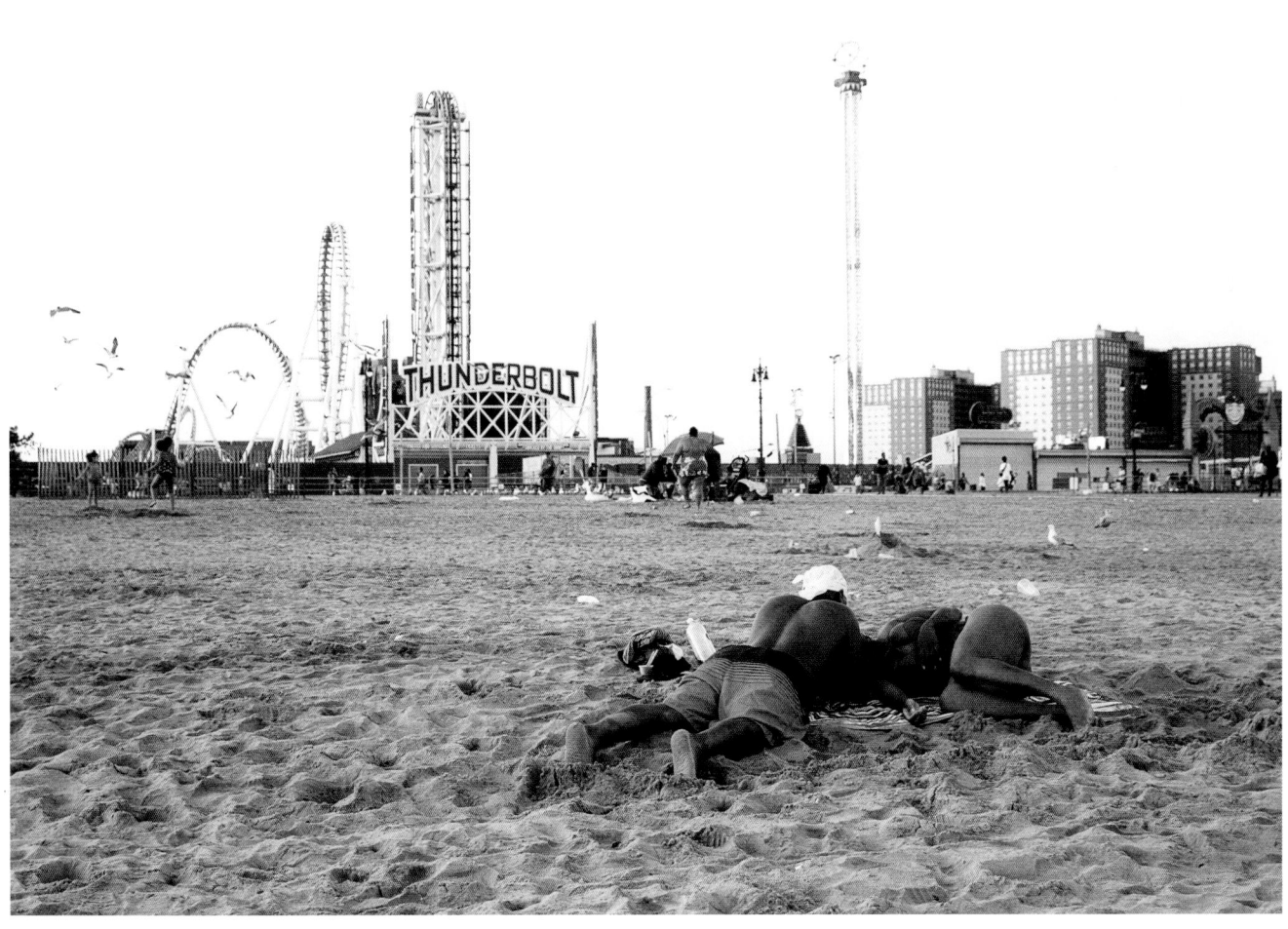

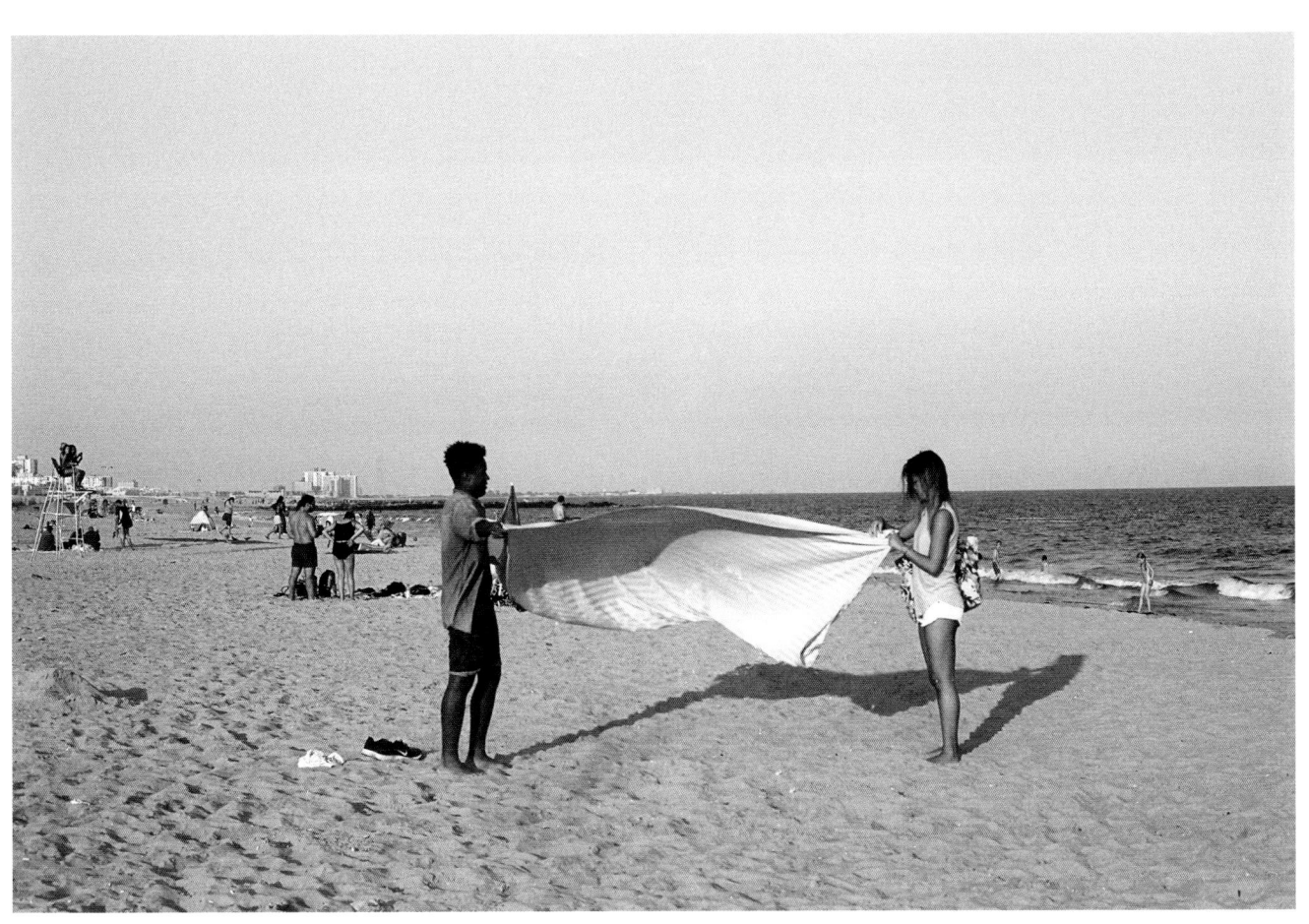

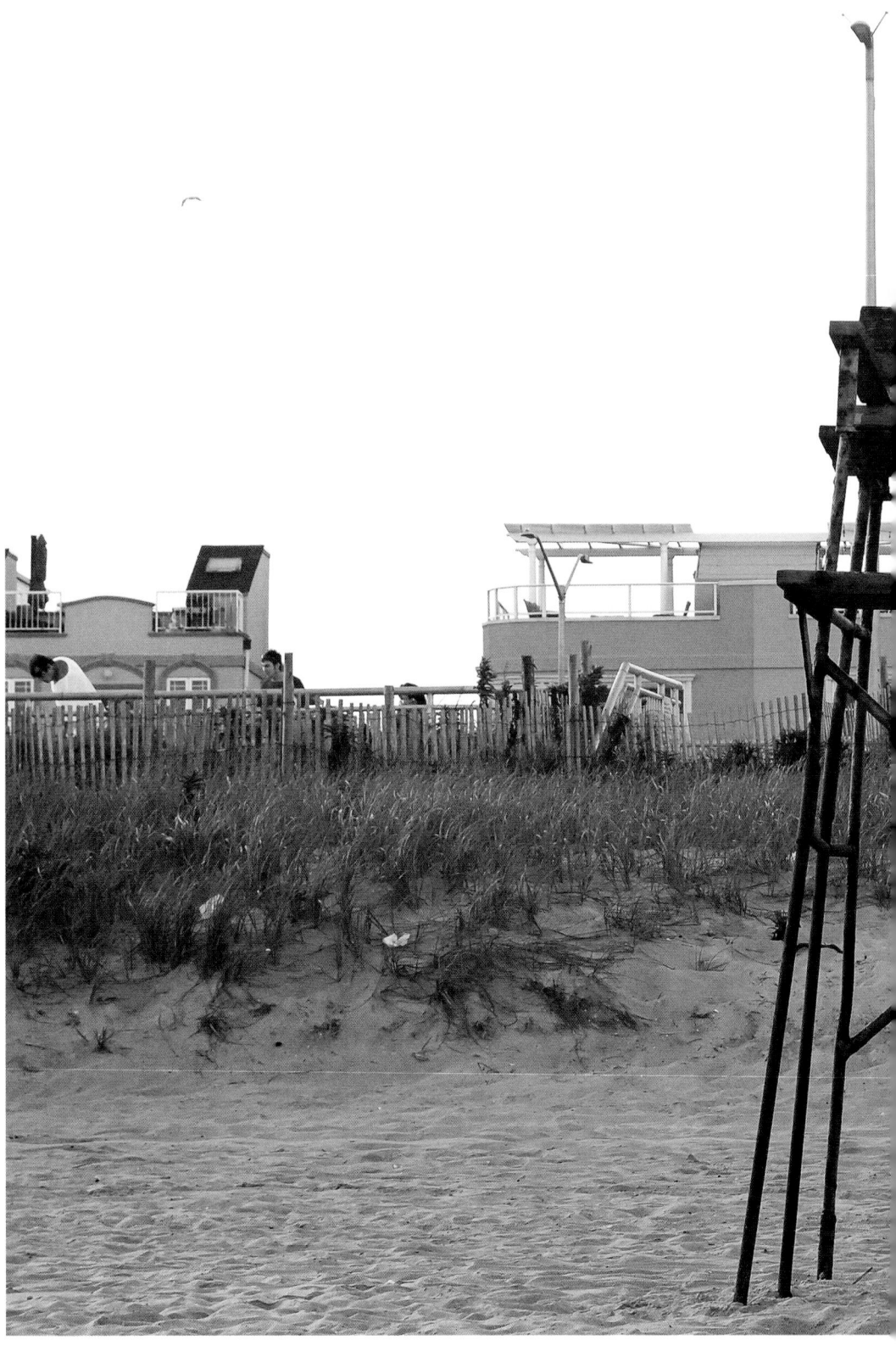

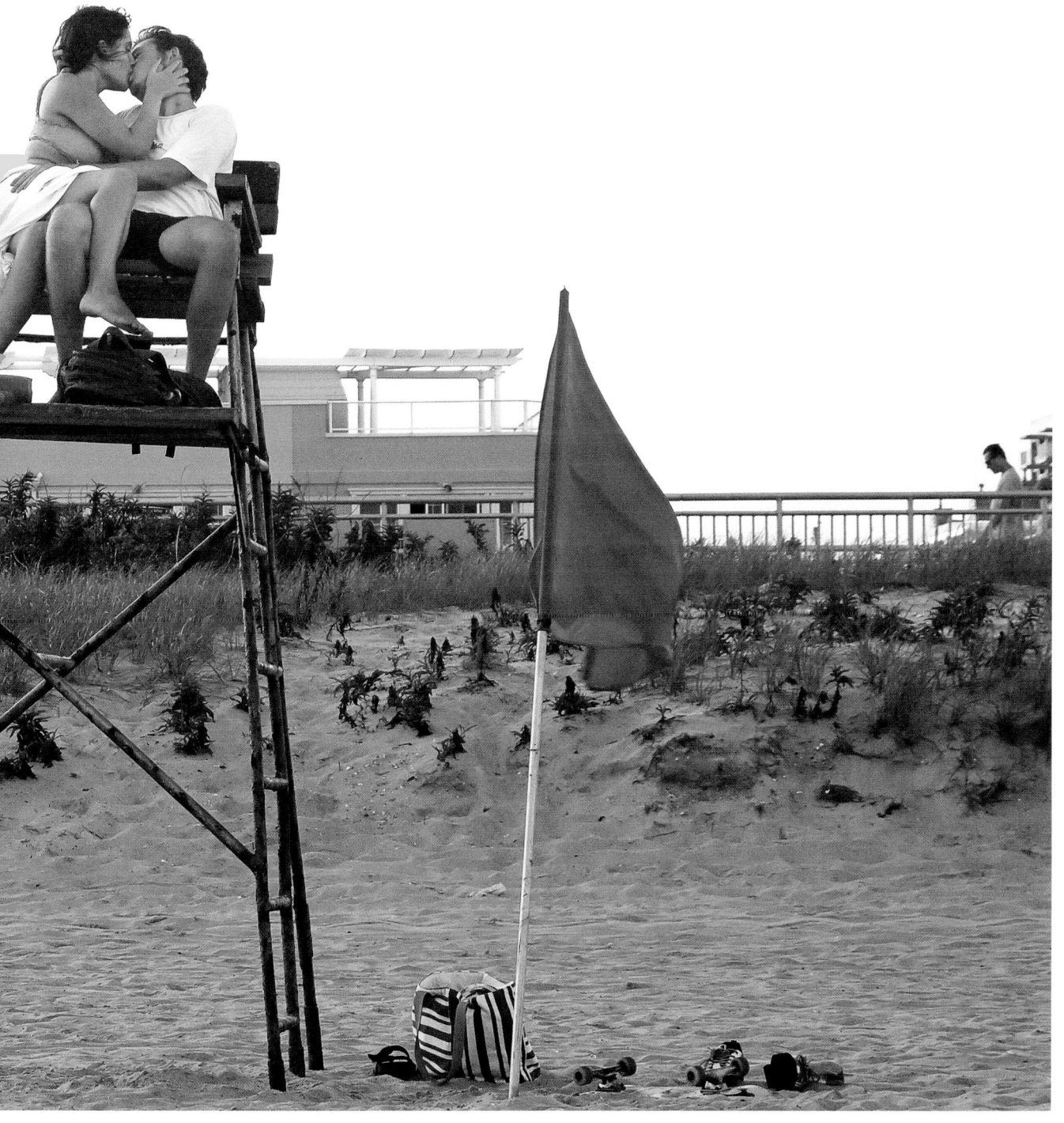

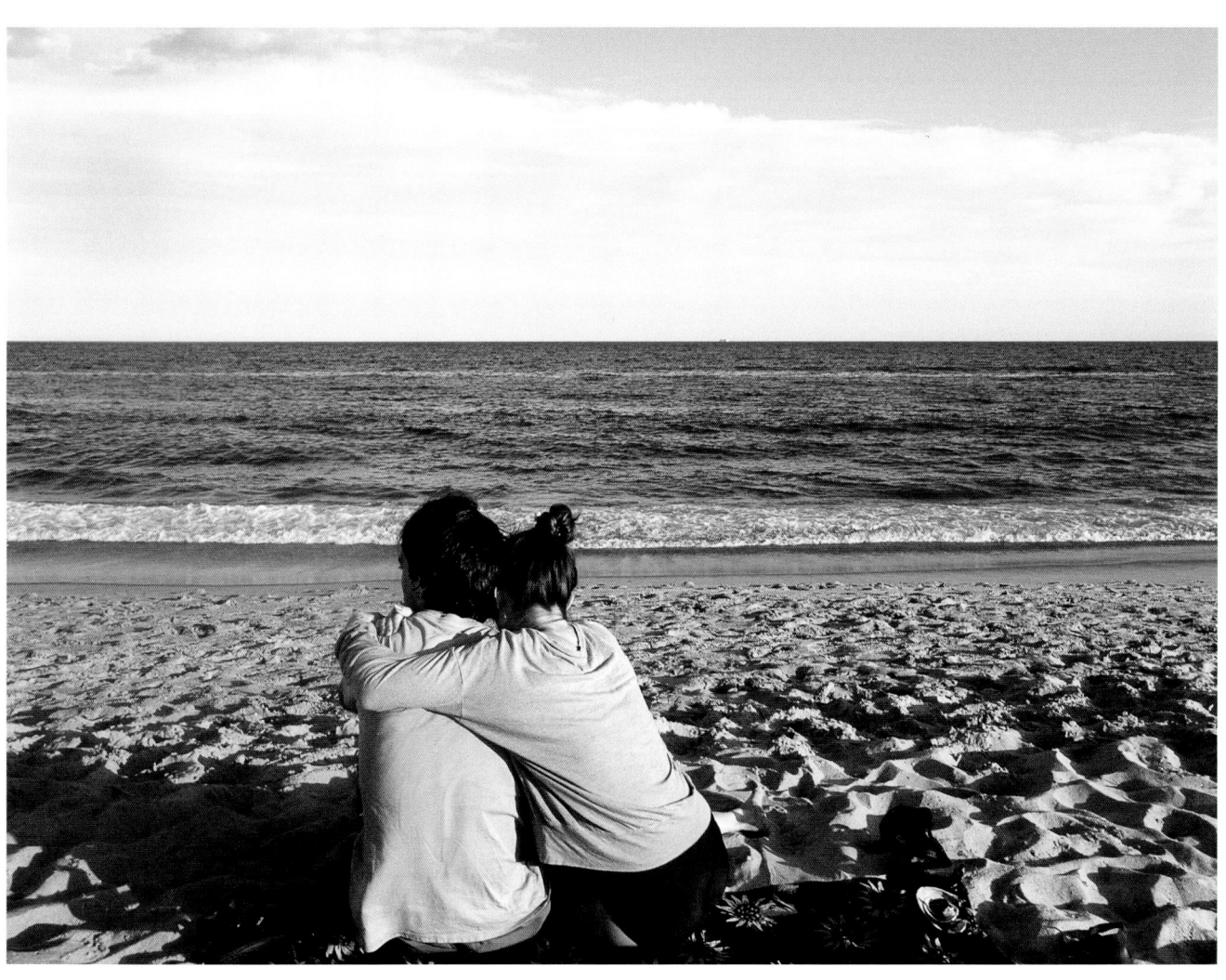

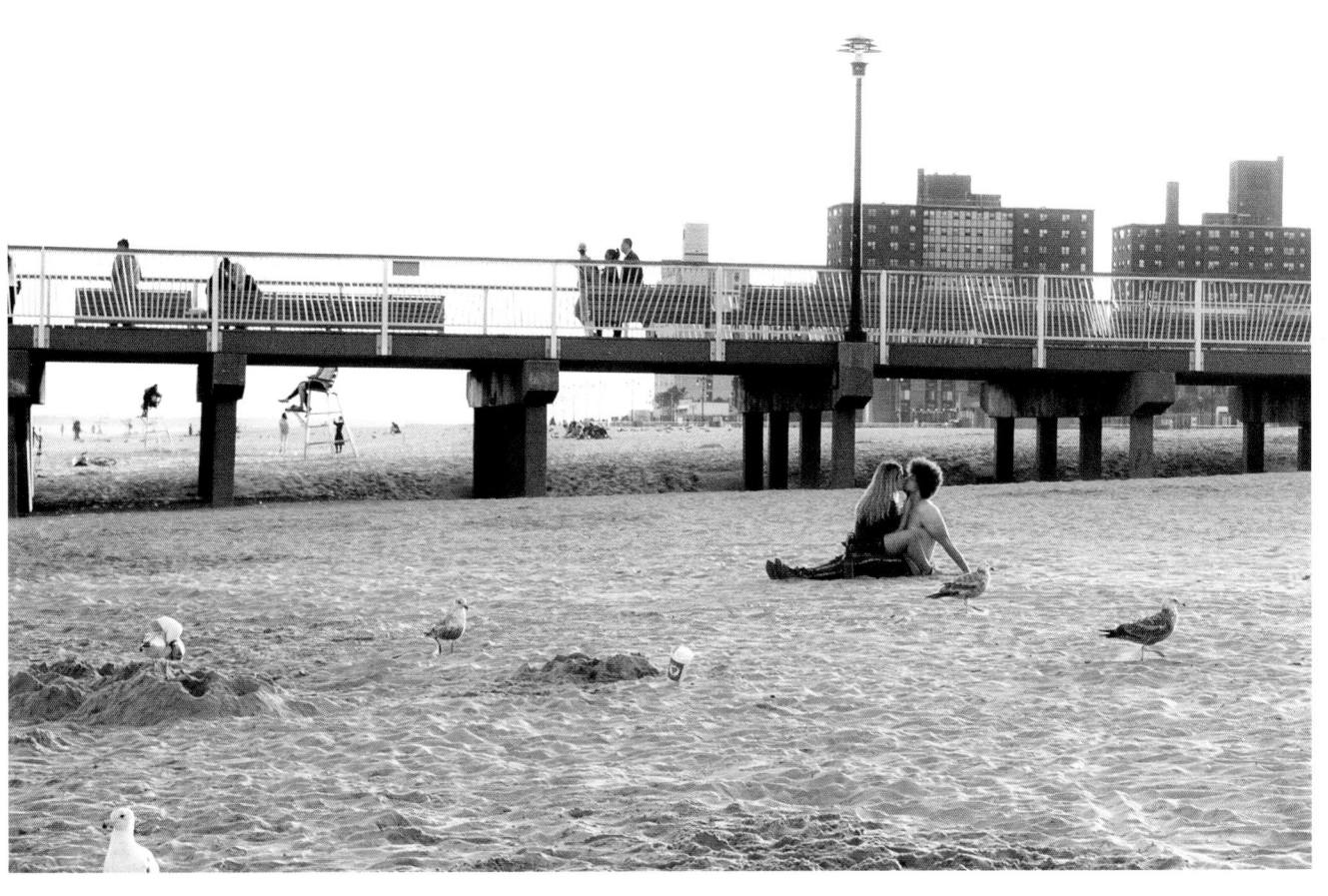

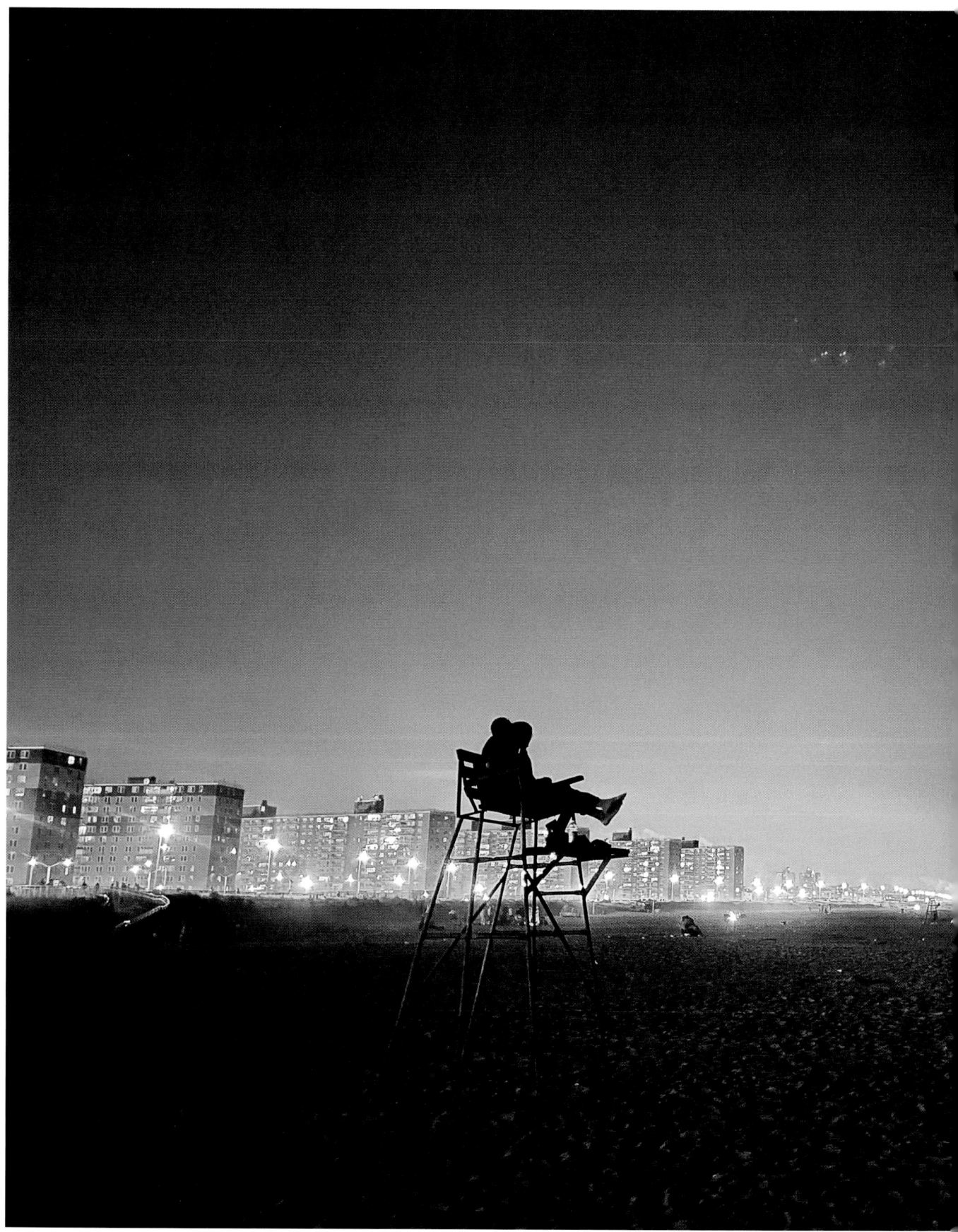

At its core, this series is about how deeply important human connection is to our survival and well-being. I've never seen people happier in New York than when they are by the ocean, with someone special next to them. This observation and discovery happened by accident.

I was soaking up my first few days of truly warm sun in late May 2015 at Fort Tilden Beach when I looked up and noticed a couple in front of me, bodies entwined. They were on their towel, reading in each other's arms and quietly holding each other while basking in the sun, not speaking (*The Silhouette*, page 103). Their quiet togetherness struck me, and I snapped a photo on my old Canon AE-1 film camera. I kept my eye out for other couples as I finished the roll in the following weeks, curious as to what else I could find.

Once I had the film developed, I was mesmerized by the results. The *Beach Lovers* series was born, and it quickly grew into an almost obsessive search. Summer after summer, I sought out all the ways in which people show each other affection on the beach, where they are so much freer and bolder than anywhere else in the city, entangled and asleep on their towels or canoodling in the water.

I became captivated by this idea of private intimacy in such a public setting. It was a thrilling challenge to bring this side of New Yorkers to light, to witness and document the beautiful range of human connection. Whether lust, companionship, or sharing a deep laugh, it is all somehow rawer and more vulnerable on the beach.

It was only a few years into the series that I admitted to myself that I was also searching for myself in this work. I'd been looking for the very connection that I hoped my photos were communicating to others. It can be easy to get jaded about love and humanity living in New York and this series gave me hope when I didn't have any. For anyone holding this book right now, I hope it does for you too. Thank you to all the Beach Lovers, and the wild and gritty beaches of this city, for this gift; this is for you.

—Erica Reade

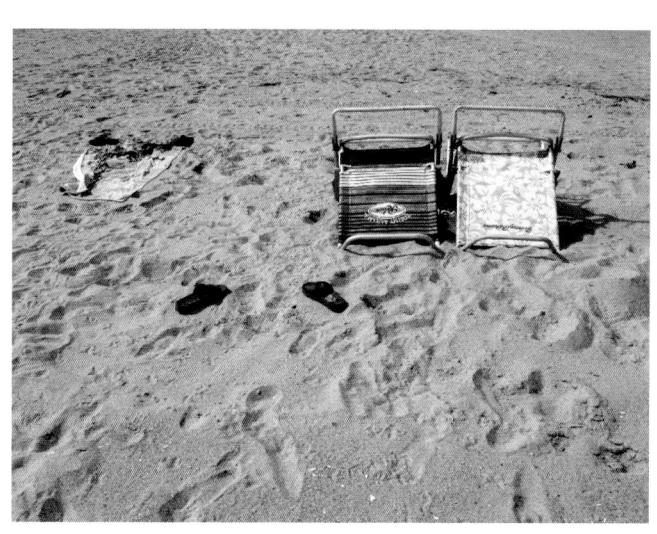

Plate List

Acknowledgments:

There are many people—too many to name all—who have supported me in making this dream of a book a reality. They include of course my family, friends, Camera of the Month Club colleagues, and the many mentors I have had along the way.

A deep thank-you to my family for all the love and support you've given throughout my life; I'm very lucky to have you all. You watched nervously as I dove into a full-time freelance life in photography just a few years ago, and this book is the beautiful fruit of my labor. I am happy to say that you can breathe a sigh of relief now. This is for you, especially for my loving mom.

A huge thank-you to all my dear friends who have supported me in countless ways, encouraging me to keep shooting this series for the last seven years, to keep believing in love, and to trust in the importance of this work. Thanks in particular to my three closest friends: Ines Bellina, whose humor, deep loyalty, and unparalleled work ethic and drive inspired me to never give up on this project; Lee Anne Vincent O'Connor, my lifelong friend who has supported my enormous growth and evolution since our friendship started; and Kendra Heisler, who never let me give up on love, even in my darkest hours. This book is for all of you too.

My sincerest thanks to Ursula Damm at Daylight Books for her incredible talent and hard work designing this beautiful book. Ursula took great care to tell this story with thought and consideration. Thanks also go to Michael Itkoff for believing in the *Beach Lovers* series and including me amongst the great talents at Daylight, a publisher I'm honored to have worked with.

And finally, I'm forever grateful to my incredibly generous Kickstarter backers: Gregor MacLean and Stephanie Hsia-MacLean, Manuela Mancioppi, Zeeshan Faruque, Frank Catapano, Yuval Brisker, Greg and Karen Arrese, Lane Sell, Lindsay Lucas, Meg Whitledge, Lynn Macdonell, Elodie Duyker, Leah Weinberg, John Wolsiefer, Kristina Libby, Diana Al Ayoubi-Monett, Stacey Polley, Scott Kalb, Shelly Potter, Lana Turner Granzo and Ralph Reade, Janet Huston, and Janice Macdonell. This wouldn't have been possible without your support and belief in my work.